TEACHING
IN A
CHANGING
SOCIETY

FOCUSING ON POVERTY AND DIVERSITY

Doris Lackey Hawkins, Ph.D.

ISBN 978-1-64468-427-6 (Paperback)
ISBN 978-1-64468-428-3 (Digital)

Covenant Books, Inc.
11661 Hwy 707
Murrells Inlet, SC 29576
www.covenantbooks.com

CONTENTS

ACKNOWLEDGMENTS

There are several people who have contributed to making this book happen. First, Dr. Kathryn McColskey is the dear friend who encouraged me to begin this journey. Next, a special thank you to my sweet husband, Brandon Hawkins, who has consistently encouraged me to "follow my dreams," no matter how challenging for him. Thank you to more dear friends: Susan Simons, Connie Davis, Susan Porth, and Cheryl Kizer for believing in me. In addition, I want to thank Lola Richbourg, lovingly known as the "grammar police" for using her expertise to make this book grammatically correct.

Finally, I want to thank Dr. Tammy Pawloski who taught me my first course about poverty and helped me to see the significant impact poverty can have on student learning.

INTRODUCTION

All That. . .and I Can't Pray?

It was a last-minute interview on a Sunday afternoon. The position needed to be filled immediately. There were three administrators sitting across the table from me. Could I do this?

"You can do this, Doris." The assistant principal encouraged. "You are an awesome teacher!"

"I can't focus. There are so many things on my mind. My heart is broken," I explained.

"We are going to add another class because we have too many students. We really need a teacher for the second grade class," the principal continued. "You have the job if you will take it."

My thoughts were racing through the many concerns of my life, from caring for a mother with Alzheimer's to an encroaching deadline on the completion of my dissertation. Things had not gone the way I had planned the last few years. As an only child, I had the sole responsibility of taking care of my mother who was usually oppositional, paranoid, and extremely depressed, as a result of her sickness. Dealing with her, her finances, ensuring that she was well-cared for, and being there regularly was demanding. Several obstacles had interfered with progress in completing the research and writing my dissertation. I had intentionally retired earlier than planned so that I could conduct research, write, and defend my dissertation. Then, I planned to go back to work. Six months after retiring, our younger son was killed in a car accident less than a block from our home. Grief was like a heavy load weighing me down every day.

As I considered all these issues in my life, I wondered why I would even consider teaching in a classroom again. I knew the demands. It had been less than a year since our son's death. Daily, I struggled just to breath as I walked the long, lonely road of grief. This was a devastating time in our life. How could I do one more thing?

Having taught in the elementary school for almost thirty years, I had many friends who were educators. With so many mixed emotions, I sought their advice. Every friend solemnly stated that I should not accept the position, except for one friend. This long-time friend and gifted educator did not hesitate when she said, "Doris, you need to take the position."

Susan and I had been friends since childhood. I trusted her completely. In my heart, I knew she was right. My wonderful husband had already said that he would go along with whatever I decided. I could see the concern in his eyes when I told him that I took the job.

Because of my experience and multiple areas of certification (to include special education), the administrators were far more confident in my abilities than I. The class I was given to manage was full of students with many, many needs. Where do I begin? I thought. Since I retired, I didn't even have classroom materials. The administrators assured me they would be provided.

That year was one of the hardest years that I ever had teaching. Almost every child in the class had special conditions or extenuating circumstance that required extra attention. The demands were great, but I asked God to guide me, help me, and strengthen me. Soon, despite the emotional drain, I realized that I cared deeply for every student in that classroom. Gradually, I found strength, courage, and wisdom in teaching these children.

Close to the end of the year, the students were given standardized testing. The results were significantly higher scores than previously. I didn't really think about it much. I just wanted the children to learn and enjoy learning.

The principal called me aside. "How did you do it?" he asked.

"Do what?" I responded.

"Get those children to improve so much." He looked perplexed as he waited for an answer.

"Oh, that. It was easy. I just prayed for each student," I explained.

* * * * *

Several years ago, I read a funny yet powerful short article about teachers. The essence of the article was that teachers are expected to accomplish an unfathomable amount of work and have many responsibilities, *yet they are not allowed to pray.* Like any effective piece of writing, this forced me to think and then really examine the role of a teacher. Having taught for over thirty-five years, I am more than familiar with the daily routine of most elementary teachers. There are many duties and responsibilities with little time. Today, while trends in education have and will continue to change, it seems the role of the teacher has only changed in increasing responsibilities and duties while allowing less autonomy.

Teaching is a wonderful profession and, throughout the years, has always attracted countless people to the profession. Now, some prospective teachers consider a job in this area as just "not an option." Between the low salary (as compared with most other professionals) and the demands on a teacher, teaching can be very overwhelming, and young people are aware of these facts. Recruiting capable young people to the profession is difficult.

Through the years, I have taught student teachers, coached student teachers, mentored young teachers, and taught education courses at local universities. For over thirty-five years, I have taught special education and elementary/early childhood education in the public school. Throughout all my interactions with students of various ages, my motives remained the same. When I was helping teachers, my thoughts were in order to help students, I must now help new teachers. Teachers have a heavy load and much to do. The responsibilities can weigh heavy on a teacher. I have seen student teachers quit, young teachers abruptly leave in the middle of the year, veteran teachers retire early, and both young and older teachers, at the end of the day, rush out of the classroom in tears. Teaching can be very frustrating.

The students in our classes today have changed. They are more diverse in the area of cultural differences, social differences, academic discrepancies, special education needs, and in many cases, language differences. These vast differences present obstacles for teachers particularly, as they try to meet the Covid 19 requirements in addition to meeting so many different individual needs. Teaching with the goal of trying to meet the needs of all students can appear to be an unattainable goal.

The truth is that teaching can be frustrating, overwhelming, and even tiring with goals that appear unattainable on a "good day." However, what keeps great teachers teaching is that teaching can be rewarding, heartwarming, invigorating, hopeful, exciting, fun, adventurous, creative, and everlasting because of the lives that are touched.

The purpose of this book is twofold. First, I want to encourage teachers and establish within each teacher personal reminders of why he/she became a teacher. Next, I hope to provide a resource for teachers with strategies that might be readily used to make teaching a little bit easier. Hopefully, this book will not only serve as a handbook and an encourager on those days when one might want to quit, but a reminder of what one person can do to make a difference, both in the individual lives of students and in the world.

Within the book are strategies for addressing some of the most challenging aspects of teaching—the students, selecting strategies that fit the students' needs, communicating with parents, dealing with time management, and coping with the demands of a changing society. My goal is to share what I have gained through life experiences, what I have learned through ongoing education (courses), and what I now understand as a result of over thirty-five years of teaching. I want to provide *facts* that are critical to building a solid foundation for teaching. To accompany those facts, I want to supply specific strategies that are fundamental to meeting the needs of specific students. In order to do this, I hope to strengthen your *faith* in God and in yourself so that you can accomplish the mammoth tasks that you will face. Finally, I want to tickle your heart with *funny* anecdotal stories that will remind you to laugh at yourself and help you see the humor in working with children who are painfully honest, naïve, and an inspiration.

A young, enthusiastic teacher full of idealism, energy, and hopefulness with no other major issues in her life would have found the class mentioned earlier to be a challenge. It didn't matter. God took a(n) (older) retired teacher wrought with grief, overwhelmed with multiple other issues, and used her to make a difference in the lives of a classroom of children. There were many challenges throughout the year, and it was not easy. However, I learned volumes that year. I grew in faith. I learned about myself, others, and God. Among my newfound learning are two facts:

- healing comes through giving (even when you think you have nothing to give), and
- all things are possible through God who will strengthen and help.

So is teaching still considered a well-respected, noble job with rewards beyond the monetary allotment and well worth the challenges involved? Absolutely! Can educators who go into this heart-tugging job find success? Most definitely! For those who are truly called, who are dedicated, and who care deeply about each student, such teachers can do it, with a little help from above. And yes, *they will need to pray a lot.*

Prayer for Teachers

Lord, help these educators who are dedicated to helping others.

Grant them wisdom, knowledge, understanding, and love.

Wisdom to see the truth, knowledge to know what to do, understanding to appreciate each student, and love to see the potential in each student.

Protect these trailblazers who tread into new areas where safety is not always present and places where they are not always welcomed with open arms.

Bless them, keep them, and help them to help others.

Thank you, for this opportunity of service.

Amen.

— 1 —

Teaching: Why Do It?

No one should teach who is not in love with teaching.
—Margaret E. Sangster

"How wonderful!" I shared sarcastically. "It's the day after Halloween, everyone is here, it's a full moon, and our class is scheduled for routine testing.

My friend and coworker smiled as she spoke, "Well, how hyper do you think the kids will be?"

Trying desperately to be optimistic, I answered, "Let's just see how the day goes. The weather is pretty. We can let them go out for recess today and get rid of that extra energy. That's a good thing."

"Well, I have recess duty and no break today. So much for going to the bathroom." She sighed.

"When you need to go, just let me know, I'll stand in the hall and watch both classes while you go." I assured her.

"I don't think I will see my class's best work on the testing today. It's just not a good day to test. I wonder if anyone looks at the calendar when they schedule these tests." I winced as I spoke.

"These children do not test well, anyway. I wish they were not tested so much. Perhaps, one thinks, 'If you test them, they will learn,' or the more you test them, the better they are?" She seemed unsure of the logic, if there were any.

"Students' test scores are how the administrators, districts, and state decide if the schools are doing well and if the teachers are doing their jobs," I grimaced as I spoke. *If the test scores don't indicate progress, then according to them, there is no progress. I know, though. These kids have made great progress!*

* * * * *

If you are not a teacher or are not in education, the conversation that I just shared may appear fiction. It's not. In addition, if you are not in education, you may never understand the dread and fear when one must go into a classroom with twenty-five elementary-age students the day after Halloween, during a full moon, on an assigned testing day, when you have no break. There is no scientific research to support the strong belief of many teachers that people and, particularly children, are very different when there is a full moon. Their emotions and attitudes appear more volatile. Sometimes, they do not complete work, cooperate, or "play well with others." They certainly do not test well.

Such days are full of energy, a lack of self-control (on the part of the students and/or teachers), and often unexpected occurrences such as visiting parents, ranting and raving about anything from wanting special consideration for their child to wanting to change the school schedule to accommodate personal plans. A student may cry at the drop of a hat, and the administrators seem to feel a strong need to catch up on evaluations/observations on that day. Everyone will agree that the day after Halloween, children will behave differently. If one considers the large amounts of sugar they may have consumed, one can count on a sugar high (which can be scientifically supported). A sugar high means high level activity. Perhaps, the teacher should have enjoyed more candy.

* * * * *

The job of teaching is demanding. The wages are not an incentive, and the summers are no longer time off as they once were. So why teach? The money is not an issue because typically teachers do not pursue education with the expectations of enormous salaries.

Usually, there are a few reasons why people become educators; they want to share their love of learning, and they want to make a difference in a child's life, or they really think the work days are shorter, the holidays are many, and that teaching is an easy job. For those who choose the latter, the rude reality of long days, responsibilities beyond the job description, and not nearly enough holidays have them running to the nearest exit within the first semester or certainly at the end of the first year. Consequently, the dropout rate for teachers within the first five years in the profession is significantly high. Presently, there is a teacher shortage throughout the country. Other than these little facts, what is the problem for teachers? Let's examine the concerns of some teachers.

Teaching is hard work

Before going into teaching, educators must know what they will encounter and be prepared to deal as many of the challenges of the profession as possible. There is a big problem as indicated by the teacher shortage. A few years ago, the rate of teacher dropout during the first five years was 50 percent. According to a more recent report (Will, 2018), the rate is 44 percent. Things are getting better and more first-year teachers entering the profession are staying. However, we still have a teacher shortage, and the salary is not the basic reason. While any employee wants a respectable salary, low salaries (compared with other professions) are not the problem. These teachers explain why they have relocated or left the profession completely:

1. *"I can no longer be a part of a system that continues to do the exact opposite of what I am supposed to do as a teacher"* (Pauline Hawkins, 2014).
2. *"Creativity, academic freedom, teacher autonomy, experimentation, and innovation are being stifled in a misguided effort to fix what isn't broken"* (Jerry Conti, 2013).
3. *"In order to attract and retain the best teachers, we must feel trusted, valued, and treated as professionals"* (Anne Marie Cargill, 2015).

4. *"I cannot continue to teach students to regurgitate information for secretive, high-stakes, standardized tests when it goes against everything I morally stand for"* (Tracey Suits, 2016).

These examples demonstrate the issue of inconsistencies among and between states regarding certification, a lack of autonomy in the classroom, the push for high test scores (at any expense), and hypocrisy in foundational philosophies by administrators (asking teachers to do something different from what is being done to them).

Before providing a more inclusive list of the reasons why teachers leave which reflect challenges in the field of education, let's examine what the Learning Policy Institute (2018) identifies as reasons to entice teachers to go to a given school, district, or state. In the August publication, the Learning Policy Institute (August 24, 2018) listed specific factors that make a state (district/school) more "attractive" for a teacher to want to teach there and increases the chance of the teacher staying. These qualities are called "teaching attractiveness." Here are a few of those qualities listed (in no special order):

- competitive salaries
- low pupil-teacher ratio
- classroom autonomy
- testing-related job security
- collegiality within the school
- administrative support

As teachers, we know what we would like to see in the classroom, and we know what we would like to avoid. Many of the positive attributes are not present in some schools, particularly low-income schools where great teachers are really needed. Once again, if I know what to expect, I can plan accordingly. These are conditions that are typical at schools in high poverty areas:

- low salary
- high pupil-teacher ratio
- no administrative support

- poor working conditions (building, furniture, supplies, heating/air conditioning, lack of modern equipment, etc.)
- lack of basic school supplies
- lack of parental support
- high number of low-achieving students
- language and/or cultural barriers
- behavior difficulties
- basic needs of the students are unmet (physical, mental, emotional, spiritual)—K. Dupere (2016) explains:

   1. *sixty-two percent of teachers say children in their classrooms are coming to school hungry;*
   2. *nearly half of all food stamps are children;*
   3. *twenty percent of food insecure families are not eligible for government assistance; and*
   4. *children facing hunger are twice as likely to repeat a grade in elementary school.*

In a great school (new building, plenty of resources, good salary, and supportive administrators), teaching is hard because of the varied needs of the students and demands on the teachers. How much more challenging is it in schools where basic items (books, furniture, heating, air conditioning, etc.) are lacking, classes are overcrowded, students are challenging, and administrators are too overwhelmed to offer much support.

So why teach?

The point is that teaching is hard at best. In addition to those reasons mentioned above, educators must maintain certification, keep up with trends and the stream of "fix all" programs, and adjust to a changing society with demands that put a lot of the responsibility on teachers. So why do those who are in education keep teaching? If it's not the money, and it's not the holidays, what is it?

If you are a teacher, take a few moments to think about these questions:

- Why did you decide to go into teaching?
- What did you hope to accomplish?
- What keeps you in this profession?
- Do you think you are making a difference in the lives of others?
- What do you see yourself doing in five years?

If you struggle with an answer to the questions, focus on the first one. What happened to make you think teaching was the profession for you? Was it your choice or that of a parent or other family member? You must follow *your dream!*

Now, think about any time in your career where your heart was touched by a student—perhaps, by what was said or done. Think about the student or parent who lovingly said, "Thank you, Mrs. [or Mr.] _____ for helping my child." If you have taught for a while, think about running into a former student only to see the student has gone on to do good things. You contributed to that success. You left your impression (either good or not so good) on the student and made a difference.

If your encounters have left you wondering how you ended up in teaching, consider real self-examination. Determine where your passion lies and what makes you smile. Go there. It may mean a slight variation from teaching into another aspect of education or another field all together. That's okay. *You must do what makes you happy.*

If the answer to any of the above questions are based on a strong heartfelt desire to teach, congratulations! Teaching is what you are called to do. You have the heart for it; God will give you everything else you need if you strive to that end and pray. The challenges that you encounter will be conquered, and you will be successful. Do not give up or get discouraged.

Teaching is a calling

Teachers who are successful have a heart for teaching and view it as a calling or commitment rather than a job. The challenges are worth the reward of responding to the call and seeing students achieve success, either in achievement and/or in self growth. These teachers do not need to be pushed to do things that are in the best interest of their students. It happens automatically. They do not need to be cajoled into meaningful, relevant professional development. They seek new ideas and learning. Such teachers strive with limitless energy and effort to help students succeed. Such teachers want students to demonstrate learning, not because of meeting a certain score but rather because they want the students to be successful. Because these teachers find learning invigorating and exciting, they feel a commitment to sharing that love of learning with students.

For those who do view teaching as a calling (as I do) and follow God's Word, it clearly states that to whom much is given, much is required (Luke 12:48). If God has blessed you with an ability to teach, He expects you to teach. You must do it as if unto the Lord, remembering that teachers are judged more strictly than others (James 3:1). As a teacher, you will influence many and have a profound impact on the lives of many. Do not take this calling lightly.

What can dedicated teachers do to overcome the obstacles and succeed?

The fact that teaching is hard suggests that teachers must be more than adequately prepared before going this profession. They must be overly prepared in knowledge and understanding of basic education practices, plan to always be ahead, and then go a step further in preparation for those things that are not expected. Here are a few specific suggestions:

- *Prioritize.* Do not forget to make time for your family and for yourself. The order needs to be God first, family, self, and job. If the correct order is not followed, there will be a breakdown in one or more areas, and you will not be successful. Be uncompromising with this. Your children will grow up fast. They need you now. Your spouse needs you now and always; be there. Other family members need you, too. Be there for them as often as you can within reason.

- *Adopt, embrace, and retain a positive attitude.* Demonstrate a growth mindset. As a teacher, you will begin trying to establish a growth mindset for your students. Before you begin, make sure you have an attitude of planned success and growth. Students will know if you do not "practice what you preach." Surround yourself with positive, encouraging people who share your beliefs and commitment. They will help you maintain a growth mindset.

- *Show your enthusiasm.* Begin each school year with excitement that is contagious and reflective of hope and eagerness to implement your new ideas and strategies to make your classroom more inviting or your teaching more effective. Show that you are looking forward to seeing the students. Change the way you set up your room. Do not use the same old way each year. It can be a representation of stagnation. As you depict growth and change, let it be reflective in what you do. Your students will see enthusiasm and be more receptive to take on that same attitude.

- *Expect the unexpected and prepare early for everything.* From the first day of school, get each task completed early.

 Get your classroom set up at least three days before the professional planning days at the beginning of the school year or three days before students begin, if there are no meetings before students start. Often, administrators will ask that new approaches or routines be used, and having the classroom set up will allow for adjusting to the new changes.

- *Make time your friend.* Time is a learner's friend and can be a teacher's worst enemy because there is a limited amount of time in each day. Students need time to take in new learning or make connections with previous learning. Begin lessons and tasks with allotted time to complete the assignments within a reasonable time frame. Consider those who work at a slower pace and those who are "fast-finishers." Plan for everything and allow extra time. Prioritize everything.

- *Set up a support system.* Work collaboratively with those within your team or other teachers in your area to save time and avoid "reinventing the wheel." Have systems in place for support with duties, students who need "time away from the class," as well as emotional encouragement and support for yourself. Teaching is not a job that works well in isolation. Teachers must rely on each other to maintain a healthy attitude and achieve success. As mentioned earlier, surround yourself with positive people. There are always pessimistic/negative people. Avoid them when, at all, possible. Give what you can to them in terms of support and encouragement and move on. Unfortunately, many negative people do not want encouragement or to change their attitudes, so do not waste your time. Remember, your time is valuable.

- *Make sure you have a hobby or something that you can invest your time in away from school.* You must have an outlet. God had a day of rest; you must have one, too.

- *Choose your shortcuts.* Some items are not as important as others. Your time is precious and limited. Papers are not people. When at all possible, work "smarter, not harder." Find ways to take "shortcuts" without compromising the integrity of your work and intentionally defying authority or shirking responsibilities.

Conclusion

Teaching is a calling. It is a difficult job in the best of circumstances and an unconquerable battle in the hardest situations. However, if God has called someone to teach, He will prepare him/her for the job. Dedicated teachers must equip themselves for the challenges of being an educator today. First, an educator begins with the right attitude coupled with prayer and dedication. Then, teachers must establish support systems that will be there when help is needed, either for encouragement or in dealing with students. Finally, those who go into the teaching profession must be lifelong learners who are always seeking new knowledge and understanding because our society is always changing. As it changes, the needs of students change. In order to meet those needs, teachers must have a collection of a collection of strategies and instructional tools to reach the diverse population that enters the classroom.

As an elementary school teacher, educators are called to an unbelievable level of competence and efficiency. They are asked to control that which is out of their control, manage the unmanageable, inspire those who are not interested, love those who are hurtful, and teach regardless of the content or the students' receptiveness to the new learning. This is a mammoth task, and I do not want to discourage those from going into teaching. I am saying there is a way to accomplish the task. However, *you will need to pray.*

"Commit whatever you do to the Lord, and you will succeed" (Proverbs 16:3)

Prayer

> Father above,
>
> Thank You for the opportunity to touch the lives
> of these students.
> Let me never forget the awesome responsibility
> and gifts that I have.
> More importantly, let me not forget the purpose
> of these gifts…
> To be used in service for others.
> Lord, there is much to do and many to serve. I
> am but one.
> Grant me wisdom to know what to do, strength
> to persevere,
> Eyes to see the truth, and love to endure.

Never let me lose sight of what is truly important.
Let my words be powerful as they are spoken
    softly in truth with love,
Let my actions be mighty yet effectively appro-
    priate in fighting for those who are helpless.
Use me through Your infinite powers to help
    these students
Embrace knowledge, truth, and the joy of
    learning.
Thank You, Lord.
Amen.

Something to make you smile

While at a gathering of friends, I hadn't seen in
    years
One asked about my life and what brought me
    cheer.
She talked of her work and all that she had done
Then, she turned and asked, what had I become?
I smiled with pride and joy, as I spoke the words
    so sweet,
"I'm a teacher, and I truly love to teach."
With envy and distaste, she quickly replied;
"Oh, you have such an easy job, I could do that,
    if I tried.
You only work till 3:00 and are off all the time.
Your job is very easy. Not at all like mine."
I took a long, deep breath, and looked into her
    eyes.
I smiled and began explaining, she seemed a little
    surprised.
"Well, I know you'd like the extras, things you
    may not know.
"Things that seem unimportant, things that
    don't really show."

It's things like morning duty, that will make one
shine.
The students come early, so you'd better be on
time.
Or the twenty-minute lunch, really you can't eat.
If you're super lucky though, you may get to
warm your seat.
You see, you have the students, they are in your
care.
Looking after them, you have no time to spare.
And you know if Johnny throws up, right in the
midst of his tray;
You as the teacher must handle it and keep other
students away.
I hope no one will get sick, that would be great.
Mary just knocked Martha's lunch off, and Adam
still has medicine to take.
Now, there's little Joseph, he doesn't like school
a bit.
Sometimes, he makes his nose bleed, or simply
throws a fit.
Recess is getting closer, perhaps a real reprise.
No, I have recess duty. That comes as no surprise.
Well, it's been three hours, and my bladder could
use a break,
But I can't go to the bathroom, there's no one for
my class to take.
The principal just called me. It's seems Jane's
mother is here.
She is very upset with me, Jane's jacket has
disappeared.
Before I can deal with that, someone just entered
my class.
The district office person has something import-
ant to ask.

Now, anyone who has ever taught knows when
    someone enters the room,
It's like an invitation for chaos to occur real soon.
Here it comes, Tom throws a fit, it seems Tamara
    looked at him.
The papers fly and then it happens, she hits him
    in the chin.
Blood is flying everywhere, Bob rushes to save
    the day.
He grabs a paper towel and then begins to say.
'Don't worry Mrs. Hawkins, I know just what to
    do.'
I'll hold him down and get Asha to hit him with
    her shoe.
Calmly I speak with Tom and explain all is well.
Then, I explain to Bob, it's time for the bell.
Thanks be to God, the bell will ring and finally
    set me free.
My deliverance is near for forty minutes, it's time
    for only me.
My, what an easy task. Teachers just have to teach.
They never worry about extras. No moneys or
    records to keep.
Teachers don't have it easy, I share without
    disgrace.
If all teachers have to do is teach; then this lady
    would have a great case.

Doris L. Hawkins

2

Essential Practices

Sharon entered the room and looked around cautiously, as if unsure of what to expect. The first day for a student teacher can be scary. Despite multiple practicums and a plethora of education courses, the first step into a classroom with so many unfamiliar faces knowing you must teach these students can be intimidating.

She looked at me and smiled. I tried to assure her that this would be a very positive experience. Her body language and general disposition told me she was shy by nature and rather timid by choice. Nevertheless, over the next few days, Sharon's manners, professionalism, and positive interaction with the students told me she had a real desire to teach and that she cared about the students.

The plan was for her to observe for a couple of days, gradually interacting with the students. Sharon took the students to related arts, lunch, recess, and had small group instructions. Gradually, she took on whole class instruction, adding one subject area at a time. She was aiming for total control of all teaching responsibilities within a week or so. She would teach a week and then begin the process of relinquishing responsibilities back to me. The last few days of her time with me, she would observe in other classes.

Her gradual assuming responsibilities was going well. It is not unusual for these young future teachers to struggle with classroom management. Sharon was no exception. As always, there were some students who were testing her far more effectively than an education course exam.

Sharon's demeanor is so mild and gentle that it doesn't appear she would really enforce any consequences for rule breaking. She would have to prove herself to the students.

As the time drew closer for her to take on more responsibility, it became clearer that classroom management was the only concern. But it was a big concern. The students were not accepting her as a teacher with authority. Her soft voice and general body language depicted gentleness and caring, but not enforcement and authority. Together with her supervisor, we talked about specific suggestions of how to improve. Sharon appeared to understand the importance of consistency and maintaining an air of confidence, but she still had difficulties. Routines must be established. Rules must be conveyed with specific consequences that are consistently enforced. She tried but continued to struggle.

Sometimes, things happen that forces a "swim-or-drown" situation. Such was the case for Sharon. Sharon was showing improvement with her management skills. However, the students were skilled in knowing how to cause her great frustration. A few days before Sharon was to take full responsibility of the class, my father became critically ill. It was unavoidable. I had to be with my father who eventually (within days) passed. I was out for over a week. Every day, I contacted Sharon to check on her and the progress of the students. Several times, she was near tears. I reassured her and pushed her to continue trying. She needed to be stern and consistent. It was a difficult experience, but Sharon survived and learned more about teaching than she would have imagined. She did gain control of the class and passed student teaching. Today, Sharon is not only a talented teacher, but also she is a veteran teacher of twenty years.

* * * * *

Teachers set the stage for learning. First impressions are part of "setting the stage." It is far more difficult to change the initial impression and rapport received by students than to just start out doing it right at first. In other words, it's easier to become more lenient than to become more strict. Sharon's experience was very difficult because she did not begin with firmness and consistency. Teachers know that it is not easy to build that special relationship reflective of a caring, supportive teacher, who enforces rules, strives to be fair, and whose goal is to do what is in the best interest for all students.

What are essential practices?

Good teachers know there is a foundation of basic teaching techniques that must be implemented to ensure effective teaching and optimum learning in all teaching arenas. These concepts are required in every classroom regardless of the needs of the students because it reaches all students. It's like a door that must be open before taking the first step toward learning. *These are essential practices.* Some say they are common sense strategies that anyone in education should know. Experience has proven that one assumes nothing. Do not assume what appears to be common sense is commonly known by all.

Excellent teachers seek out methods that have proven effective, realizing that they still may not work on every single student. However, the probability is significantly increased when the strategy has worked for most of the teachers in almost all situations. No one has time to "reinvent the wheel." More importantly, teachers are too busy identifying individual students' needs, modalities for learning, and interests to go over what has already been determined successful. Here are those fundamental prerequisites:

Set a good tone. The teacher sets the tone in the classroom. As Haim Ginott says, "I've come to a frightening conclusion that I am the decisive element in the classroom. It's my personal approach that creates the climate. It's my daily mood that makes the weather."

The teacher sets the mood. It is how the teacher reacts to various situations that will determine how the children will react. Whether it is a bug in the corner or an intruder in the building, the students will follow the teacher's lead.

We all have good and bad days. Be honest and straightforward with students. If you have a bad day, tell them and let them know you will try hard not to let it interfere with your reactions and actions. They will respect you and learn from you how to deal with obstacles and challenges when they occur.

Establish a trusting rapport with each student. This does not happen quickly. Many students have found that adults are not trustworthy. Consequently, trust must be earned through time where trustworthiness by the teacher is consistently demonstrated. Begin by showing a genuine interest in the students and what they like. At the beginning of the year, an interest survey is helpful. Remember details that are important to the student and ask him (her) periodically about those things that interest him. If the student is into sports, ask about the progress of his team, if he plays on a team. If the student likes animals, find unusual books about animals and present them to him/her. Things that bother or concern the student need to bother or concern you (to a degree). Take time to talk one-on-one to the student about those things. Go out of your way to let the student know that you care and do want to help him/her. Make the student feel special without showing partiality. Every student must feel secure, respected, and appreciated.

Provide an environment (physical classroom) that promotes and cultivates learning. The classroom is your "home away from home" and it is the same for the students. It needs to be inviting, colorful, cozy, warm, and educationally stimulating (within reason). Many teachers use soft lighting to help create the right atmosphere. Furniture arrangement, colors, rugs, wall hangings, and soft pillows or chairs set a tone that is inviting.

Use anchor charts for easy reference. They are a vital teaching aid and are necessary. Place them in an orderly manner to create a reference source and not chaos. Additional posters or pictures are acceptable if they convey information or a positive feeling. They need to be meaningful and serve a purpose. Brain research suggests too much on the walls is distracting for students. You must decide what is too much and what is enough. Ask the students for their opinions. Asking will confirm that the classroom is theirs, you welcome their input, and their opinions are valued.

Create a climate of warmth and educational stimulation. Soft lights create an ambiance that whispers peace, warmth, serenity, and security. Small lamps in selected places will do the trick. The walls need to house pertinent information relevant to the daily routine.

Students need a quick reference place for basic information. Charts for helpers, related arts schedule, progress charts, lunch count/menu, and any other general information for the daily routine needs to be displayed orderly and attractively for everyone to have easy access. This will avoid students asking the teachers questions about the routines.

Use teaching aids that are readily available for quick access. Equally as important are students having and using materials or teaching aids. Useful materials for students need to be placed so they are easy to obtain without causing distractions for others or excessive noise. Math manipulates, art supplies, writing supplies, white boards, rulers, maps, science materials, iPads, computers, and books need to be available to the students. These are tools and need to be used to help in learning. Clear explanations and expectations need to be made and established prior to using the items. A system needs to be in place so that students know the responsibility associated with using these resources. Students will not hesitate to get them when they are really needed, and they know how to return them to their proper place.

The placement of desks and the teaching table and or teacher's desk needs to be strategic. You must decide your beliefs about how students learn and let your room reflect that philosophy. If you see the value in collaboration, set up tables for students. If you want desks in a circle for discussions, set it up as such. Whether you want a horseshoe-shaped line of desks or tables, you must decide and make it happen. When you place your own seat (desk or table), remember you need to see the door at all times. This is to monitor those entering the room and leaving the room. When you are the teaching table, you need to see all other students. I always had my desk at the back of the room strategically placed so I could see all students and the door. Students' desks must be placed where all students can see white boards, smart boards, etc. Sometimes, adjustments must be made in the arrangement after school begins and use dictates effectiveness.

Build an environment of support that encourages risk-taking. Students must be willing to take a chance because learning means trying something that may or may not work or be correct. Fear of failure or ridicule will stifle creativity, risk-taking, and willingness to venture into unknown learning. Building a support system to support such action begins with the teacher. When students appear unsure of answers or what to do, guide them with hints, clues, or encouragement. If they continue to struggle, suggest they call on a friend to help. The hands go up, and a friend is called on to answer the question. It's a win-win. The initial student is a winner for calling on a friend who knew the right answer, and the friend is a winner for knowing the answer. Should it happen that a student does the wrong thing or gives an incorrect answer, smooth over the error with comments like, "I liked the way you tried to do that even though you were not sure what might be right. Let's look at it again," or "What a great learning experience!" Your reaction will guide students into a pattern of support and acceptance of all answers and actions that are not hurtful or harmful.

Establish a community of learners that support each other and view themselves as a collective unit. This will occur as a result of your actions in situations like the one mentioned above. The attitude can be reinforced through comments like, "Our classroom is a safe place where we care for each other and look out for each other. When we try to do something, it's okay if we fail because we are learning. No laughter or ridiculing is accepted. Our goal is to learn. Sometimes, learning means failing, but we will keep trying until we get it right."

Clearly communicate expectations for routines, classroom procedures, and individual conduct. The first few days of school are when these need to be addressed and established. Keep in mind, students feel secure in routines when they know what to do and what to expect. Begin with the basic expectations concerning behavior. As a class, guided by the teacher, decide what the rules or norms for conduct. Be sure all circumstances and situations are included. Include the consequences clearly stated and consistently enforced.

Many schools have programs like "Leader in Me," "Character Development and Leadership Classroom Curriculum," "Character First," "I Can Character Curriculum," "Lessons in Character," and "Values in Action." Such programs allow students to better understand appropriate behaviors and character-building attitudes. Even if your school does not have such a program, you can purchase books and implement the program yourself in your classroom. It is well worth the money and effort. These types of programs explain why actions are acceptable and reinforce positive behaviors. More importantly, there is uniformity in the expectations because everyone is doing the same thing.

Plan. Teachers need all the advantages they can get. Knowing what they are doing, where they are doing, and what is to be expected is a great advantage. Whether the planning is for a field trip, a lesson, or a visitor, teachers must have a plan A, B, and maybe, a plan C.

For example, if you plan a field trip, and a parent who is to be a chaperone does not show up. Plan *A* was for Mrs. Jones to be a chaperone. Mrs. Jones did not show up for whatever reason. Then, take the children assigned to her and split them among other chaperones. That is plan *B*.

As a teacher, I can assure you there will be situations that will not go as planned. It is so different if you are talking about just yourself; you can adjust. However, you are talking about a class of children who usually do not like changes or unexpected occurrences. Often, it can result in behavior problems. Plans can remedy the problems and ease the transition of changes.

Lesson plans can go wrong, too. Making sure you have plans that will help to make sure there is limited chaos. Experience helps to modify and adjust the lesson when needed. Still, teachers need at least a mental plan for any problems.

Always have written lesson plans, not just for the administrators, but for you. Be intentional with planning. When the lessons are written, collect all materials required for the week. Have them readily available. Be prepared for anything.

Use kid-friendly language to display daily goals/objectives and homework on the board. Then refer to each item when teaching the objective. Students need to know what is being taught and what they are expected to learn or take away from the activity. When they know the direction of teaching, they can try to grasp the new learning. Clear expectations are paramount in all situations. At the end of the day, refer back to the objectives. Determine and discuss the progress with the students. For example, "Boys and girls, you seem to have trouble with this, so we will continue to work on it."

Exit slips are an easy, fast way to assess progress. (See example in Appendix A.)

Have materials readily accessible for students and instruction. Planning is always an important component to success in teaching. When lessons are planned, collect the materials and place them for easy access. Time spent searching for materials provides opportunities for behavior problems and breaks the train of thought from the lesson. The flow of the lesson impacts on the effectiveness. Plan. Plan. Plan.

Identify the needs of each student in your classroom based on a systematic observation procedure and collaboration with supporters. Conversations with other professionals (counselors, special education teachers, speech teachers, behavior coaches, etc.) bring clarity, a different perspective, and maximum results. Particularly, those students with special needs who have multiple teachers require ongoing conversations. Collaboration with these other teachers ensures complete understanding by all and a joint effort to do what is best for the student.

Accommodate individuality. Whether teaching or testing, remember the uniqueness of each student. Variations in interests, learning styles, rates (learning and of completion of work), comprehension abilities (particularly with instructions), primary language, and modalities (visual, auditory, kinesthetic, tactile) must be considered. Teach and assess to the strongest modality. Practice with the weakest modality to improve abilities in that area. For those who are not as effective with written assessment, make sure a written assessment is practiced after the true progress has been determined. Written assessment is still the primary way to assess, and students must become as proficient as possible in mastering written testing.

Continuous feedback is critical. Throughout the day, let students know how they are progressing and where more instruction is required. Positive feedback must be part of the communication, but constructive criticism is equally as important. Students must have a clear understanding of where they are and where they are going. This provides security and gives them direction.

When encountering a situation with a student where you are unsure of what to do, use the resources of other teachers. Ask for help. Great teachers have the same goal—to help students.

Have each student involved in personal goal setting. Notebooks to represent portfolios are a good way to help students see their own goals and progress. Take time to talk with the class about the value of goals, monitoring progress, and adjusting the pace or effort to meet those goals. Use data that is available as well as developed to meet the needs of the goals and objectives. Such an approach helps each student become responsible for his/her own learning and introduces students to the idea of a portfolio or collection of information reflective of the student's growth academically and personally.

During the goal-setting, identify the subject areas of focus (usually it's math and reading) and provide assessment scores for the baselines. Discuss "typical" growth determined by the publishers of the assessment or your administration. Look at previous growth and allow the student to have a voice in the projected growth goal. Ensure that the choice is realistic, but such to stretch learning.

Maintain ongoing assessment. It is the evaluation of student progress to inform instruction particularly in regard to the particular student. Anecdotal records, checklists, conferencing, formal assessment, formative assessment, summative assessment, and teacher-made tests have their place in evaluation. Do not base overall progress and growth on one assessment, no matter how valid and reliable it may be. One testing does not represent daily progress and overall achievement.

Assess in multiple ways, at various times, through different modalities. When teaching your students, make sure you know which modality is the strongest avenue for learning for each student. When assessing, begin with the student's strength. Then, graduate to a written format because, ultimately, that is the one that will probably be used in formal assessments.

When teaching new concepts, utilize as many modalities as possible. The goal is to bombard students with the new learning using as many strategies and modalities as possible. Visual aids, auditory repetitions, active engagement, art, music, drama, written clues, collaboration, and discovery are just a few of the approaches that can be used. Discovery is a powerful strategy. Unfortunately, time is a consideration, and the time that is required for some students to make those connections on their own is too long. In these situations, use a "buddy" approach or "peer tutoring" to help the student grasp the new concept. If that does not work, you must work one-on-one and make sure the student has the foundation skills or background knowledge required to make those connections.

Plan field studies. If possible, plan field studies. There are students who do not have the same opportunities as other students as far as going and seeing things. Field studies make the learning interesting and provides firsthand experiences that will make memories.

In situations where students cannot contribute to the expense, check with your PTO and see if funding can be supplied. Sometimes, local businesses or private individuals will sponsor a student or the entire field study. Field studies are important.

Be fair. Students have a strong sense of fair play. A quick way to pave the way for trust is to be fair. Dealing with all students in the same way is not always easy, but critical. Treat each student as if he/she is your favorite (to the student). Here is a hint of what I did when dealing with students and particularly when handling a delicate situation: Ask yourself what you would do if this were your child (nephew, niece, etc.). This approach never failed me. I, soon, grew to automatically treat the children with the same love and respect that I did my own boys. For me, that is as good as it gets.

Celebrate successes. Students need to see success and learn to delight in their accomplishments. Some do not have the support at home. The teacher and classmates must be the support for these students.

The celebrations can range from little acknowledgements and positive comments from the teacher to shared congratulations from the entire class. The little recognitions include stickers, comments or goodie notes, and special privileges. Larger recognitions range from larger treats (treat box), special seating for a day, special privileges, letter/note home, certificate, and special snacks. Some teachers have a special chair for those who have met goals (read books, perfect grade on a test, significant growth with goals). Designating a special day of the week or special time is a good way to ensure that the celebration is regular and not omitted. The goal is help students see that they can achieve goals and help students appreciate the feeling of success. Some students have not experienced that thrill.

Use behavior management systems that provide a fresh start for each day. Be consistent. If the management plan is such that one day's failures carry over to the next day, the student has little or no incentive to do better because the "hole gets too deep to get out." Beginning each day with a fresh start lets students know that inappropriate actions are not remembered indefinitely. Some students may have family members who do not "forgive or forget" easily. These students are shackled to mistakes for days (or weeks). They need to know that forgiveness is provided, and new chances are given daily.

Make learning engaging (active), interesting, and meaningful. Learning can't always be fun, but it can be most of the time. Incorporate food into the mix when possible. Be silly sometimes. It's okay to laugh and enjoy the learning.

Techniques for making the learning fun stems from the teacher's attitude, enthusiasm, and overall approach. Once, I did not enjoy learning social studies or teaching social studies. Finally, I saw someone use drama, art, and music when teaching social studies. Everything changed. There are infinite opportunities to make social studies fun, from videos to plays. Remember, the fun begins with the teacher.

Connect to the real world. Take advantage of opportunities to integrate learning with activities connected to daily life. For example, write thank-you notes for visitors or those who make donations. Incorporate a writing lesson in the work

Brain-based research suggests that students need to be out of their seat about every twenty to thirty minutes, depending upon the age. Plan lessons to have students up and moving.

Utilize technology. The best teaching practices use all available strategies or techniques and tools to make learning effective and fun. Students know and enjoy using technology. There are games, resources, videos, and interactive sites that enrich activities. It is powerful in what can be done to enhance learning. If you feel inadequate about getting the most out of technology, take courses or ask friends to assist you. You need to be very knowledgeable about the advantages and disadvantages of technology. Young children learn quickly how to find inappropriate sites. Monitor the use.

Set the foundation for new learning. Before a new concept can be processed by a learner, there must be a connection with previous learning. If students have not had any previous learning to build upon, the teacher must provide it. Know the students well enough and do preliminary evaluations to determine those who will need more experience or understanding as a foundation for the new learning.

Be creative. As long as the children are actively engaged, interested, and are making connections, try new ideas to teach the concept. Bring in artifacts, props, food, people, and things to make the learning more fun.

Use humor. Humor makes teachers more human. Do not be afraid to share silly experiences or share those that include your family. In doing so, students will see that you have a normal life and love your family. It solidifies the idea that you are a nice person. Set up situations for laughter (at appropriate times). Perhaps, the most effective tool to decrease stress and provide enjoyment in learning is laughter. Use funny read-alouds and look for humor in everyday situations; share those funny moments from your family with the class.

Use collaboration. Collaboration is such a wonderful way for children to share learning. Like so many other things in education, there is a time and place for all things. New learning invites discussions, sharing, and provides for those reluctant students to hear, watch, and then share without fears.

Review frequently. Reviews should be done in such a way as to review the material by presenting it in a different context. Use it in authentic situations; it will be more valuable and improve the learning.

Maintain, nurture, and promote parental involvement. Help the parents develop a partnership with the teacher as advocates and support systems for their students. Ongoing communication through technology as well as weekly paper newsletters is important. Periodically, send a positive note praising a student (particularly to the parents of those who struggle to demonstrate self-control). Help parents develop a partnership with the teacher as advocates and support systems for their students.

Be a great role model. Be cognizant of what you say and do. Model appropriate social interaction with students and other teachers. Eyes are always watching.

Conclusion

Some strategies and approaches to teaching are questionable in their effectiveness for all students. Some are like fashion. They come and go. There are some practices that are proven through time to be good methods. Research reveals there are practices that are consistently effective in teaching. These techniques are the foundation on which great teaching can be constructed. As always, it begins with the teacher. The teacher must be dedicated to the task of lifelong learning for him/herself and committed to doing what it takes to ensure all students learn.

The teacher's attitude must be positive with a growth mindset, establishing an environment for learning and success on the part of all students. Communication is the next primary element among the basic tools for teaching. Clear, consistent, communication is paramount and must be provided for both students and parents. A trusting rapport with students and parents must be established and maintained. Regular assessment integrated throughout the routines is important to inform the teacher of student progress and to drive instruction. Teaching through students' strengths and building up their weaknesses is accomplished when teachers know the students well so as to identify these traits. Planning well, making learning fun and meaningful, varying the activities, engaging the students, providing an environment that enhances learning, and using humor makes for effective teaching. It's up to the teacher to make it happen, and *you will need to pray.*

Prayer

> Lord,
>
> While children are so very different, they are all human.
> Humans need love, encouragement, hope, security, and reassurance.
> Provide me enough of these to give generously to each child.
> Help me use the fundamental approaches that are effective with all students
> In such a way as to let the students know I care, and they can succeed.
> Thank you, Lord.
> Amen.

Something to make you smile

Molly had a heart for teaching. She taught for many years, knew her content, and had great classroom management skills. Her enthusiasm and love of her students was evident in all that she said and did. So much so that daily, she put aside time to share some of the many adventures of her own life or those of previous students. Her students loved her and her stories.

One day, Molly walked over to the stool to begin a new story. She looked across the room at the class of third graders eagerly waiting to absorb every word of a new adventure. Molly climbed up on the stool and positioned herself. She squirmed a little, situating her short legs on the lower rungs of the stool. The skirt she wore hung slightly below her knee. She pulled at it to maintain modesty and still be comfortable. The students were ready with pencils down and full attention on her. Finally, she was ready to begin.

As she shifted her foot to ensure a secure seat, Molly glanced at the class to see the children's eyes locked on her every move, and she began the story. "Not long ago, when my boys were young..." Suddenly, her words stopped and were replaced with "ah oh-h-h-h." The stool began to tilt, and her legs went out while her skirt went up. Despite her efforts, her sixtyish body would not cooperate and do what she wanted it to do. Gravity won. Down she fell with her legs open and her skirt over her head. Modesty was lost as all was revealed. Molly could not feel the aches throughout her body because of the overwhelming embarrassment she felt. Trying to regain composure and decorum, she sheepishly looked out at the class.

While most of the children stared with great astonishment filled with a concern for the well-being of their teacher and embarrassment at seeing too much, one little boy in the front row felt compelled to cover his eyes and eliminate any future guilt of having seen that which should not be seen. It was quiet, and then, he calmly asked, "Is it okay to look now?"

3

Poverty

Another truck is full of things to take to Scarcity (not the real name). The church collects goods from its members, loads it on to the U-Haul truck, and then, it is driven to a part of the state with many low-income families. The items include used clothes, furniture, household goods, toys, and anything else that the church members do not want but feel may be used by others. Once, a toilet was donated. Some of the church members wondered if that was an appropriate item to put on the truck. When the truck arrived, people fought over it. The church has been donating to this community for years now. The need is never satisfied.

* * * * *

Whether pushing a grocery cart or carrying a small bag of belongings, the homeless are everywhere. Every Saturday, a meal is served in the down-town area of the city. Several local churches participate in the program to feed these homeless people. Sometimes, clothing, books, rain gear, blankets, and personal hygiene products are passed out. Always, there are many people (one hundred fifty to two hundred) standing in line. Those responding are old, young, and of different races and appearances. Once, there was a preg-nant woman. Sometimes, there are children there. The number of people who are fed varies, but they always come back. The need is always there.

* * * * *

Some families are desperately trying to get out of homelessness and are on their way to finding homes. An organization has been formed by local churches who work together to house families as they are in transition from homelessness to permanent homes. Each week, a different church provides these families shelter, food, and transportation until the final arrangements can be made for their homes. Some will find homes and move on. However, another family will take their place waiting for a home. The need goes on.

* * * * *

These examples are real and depict situations where help is being provided, but solutions to the problem are not being found. Poverty is a complex problem that profoundly affects individuals, families, schools, communities, states, and countries. The problem is not unique to just one city, state, or country. Everywhere, there are people in desperate need of food, shelter, clothes, and other necessities for survival.

What is poverty?

Poverty is the lack of resources required for normal growth and development. Those basic resources include items that meet physical needs (food, shelter, clothes, water), mental needs (mental stimulation), emotional needs (love, security), social needs (healthy interaction with others), and spiritual needs (expectations to find meaning and purpose in life). Throughout this book, reference to poverty refers to someone who may lack one or all of the above-mentioned items. The focus of this book is directed toward teaching children in poverty. In order to understand the challenges they may face, one must understand poverty and how the government defines those who live in poverty.

It is hard to believe that there are children who are homeless. Some are living in cars or temporary shelters. The Department of Housing and Urban Development defines homelessness as a person living or sleeping in a place that is not meant for human habitation or living in a homeless emergency shelter. There are levels of homelessness beginning with "literally homeless," "imminent risk of homelessness," "homeless under other federal statues," and finally, those "fleeing/attempting to flee domestic violence" and as a result are homeless. The range of homelessness goes from those who are temporarily without housing to those who have been homeless for more than one year. The latter category are those people (including children) who are in extreme poverty. The number of people in extreme poverty are increasing within the United States.

According to US Department of Housing and Urban Development in 2018, over half a million people in the United States were homeless. This number represents seventeen percent of the population and includes children. These people are living in cars, streets, or one-night homeless shelters (emergency shelters). Over two hundred thousand of these people were families with twenty-five percent of the group being children.

Aside from children, those who have chronic homelessness and make up a small percent of the total group of homelessness tend to have behavioral health problems, severe mental illness, and substance abuse. In addition, they may have physical illnesses, injury, and/or trauma.

California is an example of the chaos that the crisis of poverty can have on a community. Twenty-five percent of the nation's homeless people live in California. As of January 2018, according to US Department of Housing and Urban Development (HUD), there were an estimated 129,972 people living in horrific conditions on the streets in several cities in California (Los Angeles, San Francisco, Bakersfield). These people were living in tents, under benches, along the streets, and on the lawns in various public places. It has become a health crisis. These people have no bathrooms and garbage service. There is an outbreak of various diseases including hepatitis and a concern with rodents. In ordinary situations, homeless people are more susceptible to common communicable diseases such as influenza, strep throat, gastroenteritis, sexually transmitted diseases, HIV/AIDS, and tuberculosis. Such toxic situations as in California increases the health risk to the homeless and to others.

Ben Carson, secretary of Housing and Urban Development, on a news program (2019) addressing the problem of homelessness in California, explained that allowing the people to live on the streets in tent-like structures is not really showing compassion. Compassion means helping the homeless become self-sufficient and not have to live in such unsanitary, unhealthy conditions. Dr. Carson goes to the heart of the problem when he explains the people who are homeless are there for three basic reasons: drugs, mental illness, or hard luck. While the solutions are not easy, solving the problem must begin at a local level. Then, those who initiate action can call upon state agencies or federal funds to assist.

According to the 2018 US Census Bureau, about 12.8 million American children (below the age of eighteen) live in poverty. While that is an improvement from the 13.3 million children living in poverty in 2016, the number is unfathomable. The United States is not only a leader in the world, but also, it is one of the richest countries in the world. Nevertheless, we have a significant problem.

Types of poverty

Poverty is not just the absence of finances required to provide food and shelter. It can be a lack of attention to medical (physical) needs, emotional concerns, or social needs from parents (or caregivers) as a result of neglect, indifference, or unconcern. Teachers usually have access to information that will help distinguish between those who cannot provide and those who do not provide for their children. Guidelines are in place at most schools for teachers to contact those who can help children who are being neglected or abused. Those who are being neglected are still those in poverty because their basic needs are not being met. It is important that teachers do not limit identification of those students lacking basic needs to just those without financial resources.

My goal is to help teachers help children. The only time the cause is pertinent is when something can be done to change the cause. Otherwise, the goal is to meet the needs of the student. Often, symptoms can be similar for situations with different causes. A student who needs help is a student who needs help. The first step is always to demonstrate care and concern to offer help.

The level or degree of the impact that poverty has on a child stems from the length of time he/she lives in those conditions, the type of poverty, and the individual. There are six types of poverty based on the level of poverty and the length of time one may be in poverty:

- *Generational poverty* is poverty that is passed down from one generation to another. It becomes a "way of life" and, in some cases, is just accepted by the family members. The challenge with this type of poverty is that it's like trying to dig out of a hole. Digging just makes more dirt, and the hole gets deeper. The one way out is with education, determination, and opportunities.

- *Absolute or extreme poverty* is defined by the government as those who live on less than half the poverty level income. Daily survival is focused around meeting basic needs of running water, shelter, and food. Just trying to live is a challenge for this group of people. Getting out of this level of poverty is almost impossible without great intervention.

- *Relative poverty* is a type of poverty identified by a comparison of income to the average standard of living in a person's society. Such a label only serves to identify those who are living below the average standard of living. The level of living can vary from slightly below the average standard to significantly below. Education, opportunities, and great determination can aid someone out of this type of poverty.

- *Urban poverty* occurs in areas with populations over fifty thousand. Typically, violence, noise, overcrowding, and little or no community help services are available. The lack of services makes it extremely difficult to get out of this type of poverty.

- *Rural poverty* is typically seen in smaller areas with populations below fifty thousand. Because of the limited size, there are limited opportunities and services for help. Once again, it is difficult to get out of this situation.

Some of our youngest children (below five) have the highest poverty rate of nearly one in five toddlers lacking required resources during the time of greatest brain development. As mentioned earlier, the length of time that a child is living in poverty is directly related to the degree of adverse trauma left behind with the child. Some children are in and out of poverty on a regularly basis. If that is the case, then it's only the length of the current "situational" poverty that is relevant for the child. If this term is while the child is in extreme poverty, that is very different from a term of moderate poverty. The levels of poverty are significant in the effect it has on developmental milestone and emotional or social devastation for the child. Regardless, poverty will have long-lasting influences on the child throughout adulthood. Being hungry and without a place to stay is a condition that is not easily forgotten.

Helping those in poverty

Helping those in poverty or people who are living in conditions where they lack the basic needs is a problem that is complex because the causes for the problem are varied, and funding is not readily available. Whether it is a case of mental illness or drug abuse, these people need help. Sometimes, people just have hard luck, or they have given up on life and society. For some, the situation can be a cycle of drugs, money for drugs, crime, violence, and self-destruction. For others, it can be a struggle from one day to the next to survive. In either case, the problem is being perpetuated or pacified rather than solved, or it's being totally ignored.

Attempts to make it better need to be guided by thoughtful mental consideration rather than a quick emotional response. First, we must help others to recognition that poverty is a problem. Then, we need people who want to help. Lastly, we need to unite in a commitment to make a difference by attempting to do something to make it better. We begin with caring people.

Teachers can do only so much to help the concern of poverty. They can address situations within their classrooms. They can be great leaders within the community. However, It is up to society to seek assistance and solutions. After recognition of the problem, solutions should be designated based on needs. It begins with identifying those who are dealing with "hard luck" situations from those who are suffering mental illnesses and drug addictions. Unfortunately, within the mix may be those who do not want any change. Regardless, housing needs to be provided with knowledge and resources to:

- help the mentally ill;
- detox the drug addicts/alcoholics; and
- find temporary housing for those dealing with "hard luck."

Permanent solutions can be given through training or education for all three groups. For those dealing with mental illnesses, a doctor must determine their needs. Detox patients need a program to support them and teach them how to deal with their problems. Finally, those dealing with poverty as a result of more temporary situations need to know what to do to get out of the situation so they can become a contributing member of society (specific skills and education). Then, help needs to be given.

- Classes for parents needing assistance in money management could be offered by the school.
- Classes for devising a plan of action to get out of debt could be offered.
- Budget shopping and priority setting classes or guidance.
- Churches must reach out to those who are in need.
- Community leaders must recognize those in the area who are lacking resources and seek to establish assistance.
- Business owners can work collaboratively to make accommodations for those in need.
- Individuals can become more aware that there are those who do not have enough to meet their basic needs and determine how to help.

- Society can make a difference if individuals unite in a joint effort to help those within the community who are in need.
- Many may see the problem as one that is too overwhelming for an individual to be able to attempt. Small steps in the right direction can begin an effort that could result in an avalanche of people on board to find a solution and make a difference. Here are a few specific things that can be done to help the cause:
- Identify community leaders. Have conversation to make them aware of specific needs.
- Contact local politicians to determine present policies regarding poverty. Find out what can be done to improve the situation.
- Solicit help from local organizations that are established to offer help and support to those in need.
- Develop and maintain a running list of agencies in your area that can help those in need.
- Talk with your politicians and be specific with your suggestions for help. The Center for America called for congress to do the following:

1. create jobs
2. raise the minimum wage
3. increase earned income tax credit for childless workers
4. support pay equity
5. provide paid leave and paid sick days
6. establish work schedules that work
7. invest in affordable child care
8. expand Medicaid
9. reform the criminal justice system
10. avoid cuts to programs that support those who need help

While teachers are limited in what they can do, they can try to encourage the community to have a voice. Each person must make his/her congressman aware of any of the above listed ideas that you accept and want to have implemented.

Dr. Carson (mentioned earlier) suggests the solution begin at a local level. I agree. From the perspective of an educator, providing solutions is even more difficult because we have limited power. Our priorities are the students who enter the classrooms. Teachers must strive to meet the primary needs of these children before secondary needs can be met. Then, other resources can be provided to include the education of parents to help find a permanent solution.

Because children cannot help themselves, they are the priority. Children of poverty cannot get out of poverty by themselves. The result of poverty on them is life-changing. It is up to society to identify and unite in obtaining solutions. The way society treats children are reflection of a country's heart and future. These children are vulnerable, blameless for their present state, and are the mercy of others. They must be protected and helped. Reaching out to the children is really the only significant impact teachers can make on those who live without necessities. Teachers can make a difference.

Teachers lead the way

Teachers can be the bridge for students between hopelessness and hope, fear and confidence, failure and success. Students are looking for someone who will find the unique qualities in them and celebrate those extraordinary skills and talents they do not even know they possess. It does not matter if the students are rich or poor, gifted in the academic areas or not; all students want someone who cares about them and sees something special in them. Some students need this more than others. Certainly, children of poverty need a teacher who will show them the way to better things and give them a reason to try.

Teachers can contact professionals who can offer support and provide resources for low-income families. Guidance counselor usually have access to help in the sense of clothing, medical care, or food packages. Many schools collect coats to pass out during the winter months for those who do not have them. Local churches have programs that sponsor or help those in need. The teacher is often the only one who can act as a liaison between the lack of resources and a source for supplying those resources.

Conclusion

Our society is ever-changing. In the midst of all the changes, educators are expected to meet the needs of all students, regardless of their different cultures, academic levels, socioeconomic backgrounds, and varied learning styles. In the past, most education books addressed all these aspects of teaching except possibly helping young teachers prepare for the ongoing changes and the present challenge of meeting the needs of children in poverty. The causes of poverty (while varied and very complex) are not the first concern of teachers in helping these students. The priority is realizing that students will be unable to function at their best when they lack primary necessities (food and clothing). They need their basic needs to be met first. Then, teachers can approach the children along with the problems they bring into the classroom.

Meanwhile, teachers, in collaboration with the school, must provide avenues for the parents to take that will begin to get them on the road to recovery and not just "place a bandage on a major wound." Like the children, the parents have primary needs that must be met first. Then, they need skills for better jobs and guidance on how to take action/assistance to get out of poverty and stay out of the spiral it can create.

Children in poverty are more likely to have academic difficulties, physical problems, and mental/social/emotional challenges depending on the type of poverty and length of time being in poverty. These children need to be able to begin their education with their fundamental needs being met.

The second issue is the recruitment of good teachers. According to the latest research, the teacher is the most influential factor in the process of educating our students. Great teachers will know how to focus on the needs of students and then begin to meet those needs and educate the students. Great teachers will find resources, determine best practices, and make do with what is available.

While recruiting good teachers is the job of school districts, state departments of education, and colleges/universities of education, meeting the needs of the students is the job of the teacher—to a degree. The teacher cannot provide the students all of the basic needs of food, shelter, clothing, clean water, medical care, security, appropriate social interaction, and emotional/mental support. Children of poverty are lacking one or more of these items. The results of poverty can be developmental delays, academic difficulties, social difficulties, emotional problems, and health issues. From the onset, students of poverty must catch up with peers, function as if their needs are being met, and do so while working at a great disadvantage.

Solutions begin with awareness of the problem by society, as a whole. Individuals must lead the way in providing a means for these people who do not have enough. Leaders in the community must be challenged to pave the road to making more opportunities and making connections between those who need and those who can help. Many voices will be heard and will not be ignored.

> *"Being unwanted, unloved, uncared for, forgotten by everybody, I think that is a much greater hunger, a much greater poverty than the person who has nothing to eat" (Mother Teresa).*

There are many people who lack resources in our world. The best that we can expect is that we, as teachers might touch their lives in such a way as to make a difference. That can only happen when we ask God to help us through prayer; *you will need to pray.*

Prayer

> Lord, make me an instrument of Thy peace;
> Where there is hatred, let me sow love;
> Where there is injury, pardon;
> Where there is error, the truth;

Where there is doubt, the faith;
Where there is despair, hope;
Where there is darkness, light;
And where there is sadness, joy.
O Divine Master,
Grant that I may not so much seek
To be consoled, as to console;
To be understood, as to understand;
To be loved as to love.
For it is in giving that we receive;
It is in pardoning that we are pardoned;
And it is in dying that we are born to eternal life.
Amen.

St. Francis of Assisi

Something to make you smile

Praying is an important part of our lives. We pray regularly.
Our youngest son (about five at that time) and I sat down to enjoy lunch. I looked over and reminded him, "Ashton, we need to pray."
Looking pensive at first, Ashton turned to me with questioning eyes, and he asked, "Mom, do you ever think you bug God?"

4

The Impact Poverty Can Have on Learning

Jane looked different. Her clothes were dirty, and her hair uncombed. No one really noticed that because of the dark scar on her face. She was different. She was tall and didn't talk much. In class, none of the other students wanted to be close to her. Some students seemed afraid of her. The teacher spent a lot of extra time with her. She was different.

* * * * *

Tom walked into the class long after the bell rang. He was late as usual. His hair appeared uncombed, clothes wrinkled and soiled, eyes heavy as if half-asleep. The other children hardly noticed his entry because he is usually late, and he dresses the same. Slowly, he placed his bookbag on the hook, took out a book, and walked over to his desk. Unaware of the other children working hard, Tom opened the book and began to read. Reading was his solace and refuge. He was in his world because his world was difficult. Besides, he knew he was different.

* * * * *

Children lacking basic resources to grow and develop often do make students appear different. Sometimes, those basic needs are food and shelter. Other times, those basic needs are care and guidance which includes attention to physical needs (bathing, sleep, medical care). In some ways, these students are very different. Not in feelings and needs. We all need food, shelter, mental stimulations, social interaction, emotional support, physical care, and most of all, love.

Both stories depict real situations. Both children know they are not received well by the other children. Both children have their own way of coping with the situation. The difference is that one occurred about sixty years ago, and the other happened two years ago. Have we made real progress in addressing the needs of all children? Is poverty the same now as it was sixty years ago? What is the problem?

There's a problem

The problem is children who lack basic resources important to healthy growth and development and the huge impact it can have on learning. Lacking these basic resources associated with those being in poverty can cause developmental delays, impair the growth and development of the various parts of the brain that effects memory and is used in readiness, shut down positive emotions which directly influence higher order thinking, and stunt the growth of emotional intelligence which is directly related to success in school. Not all children living in poverty are doomed to learning difficulties, but they are at a higher risk. Intervention can bring about a change.

Living in poverty is as prevalent today as it was sixty years ago and continues to rob children of opportunities to grow and becoming happy healthy adults. Children who lack the fundamental resources that are critical for living, growing, and developing are at a disadvantage physically, mentally, emotionally, and socially. At time, these learners are identified by peers as being "different" and then ostracized making the problems of poverty more severe. The effects of poverty on learning and, more specifically, on the brain presents real problems for learning. Here are some of those impacts:

- *Short-term and long-term memory loss.* The detrimental effect of poverty on child development clearly reveals that stressful or traumatic life events have a significant impact on short-term and long-term memory for those who grow up in poverty.

- *Smaller gray matter in the brain.* The gray matter (part of the brain directly involved in readiness skills) for a child growing up in poverty is significantly smaller than developmental norms.
- *Lower test scores.* As much as 20 percent of a gap in standardized test scores for children of poverty compared with other children is on average, children from low-income households scored four to seven points lower on standardized tests. As much as 20 percent of the gap in test scores could be explained by maturational lags in the frontal and temporal lobes.
- *Impact as early as infancy.* The harmful effects of poverty on children has been identified as early as infancy.
- *School readiness.* Poverty is directly linked to structural differences in several areas of the brain related to school readiness.
- *School dropout rate.* Students of poverty are five times more likely to drop out of high school than high-income students (Rumberger 2009).

The problem is poverty and those things it can bring to children. In addition to such challenges as high mobility, homelessness, hunger, food insecurity, one or more parents not in the home, domestic violence, and drug abuse, learners must correct the damage that has been done to the brain as a result of living in the condition of poverty. In other words, the brain must be rewired to accommodate and allow for new learning.

What can teachers do?

While the impact of improper diet, stress, and a lack of basic resources on learning is not new information, recent research has given new hope and insights to correcting the damage to the brain, done as a result of conditions that can be the result of poverty. Educational neuroscience takes what is known and understood about the brain and applies it directly to education. This new perspective to learning and growing the brain has emerged and continues to grow. Unlike the understanding of long ago, the brain can change. We understand that actions, attitudes, and new learning can grow the brain. Plasticity or changes in the brain as a result of experiences is a fundamental concept utilized when trying to help children of poverty.

Learning is the ability to quickly reactivate the chemical communication between neurons (nerve cells). "The more a network of neurons fires together, the more likely they are to fire together again over the long term" (Zadina, 2014, p. 16). In other words, the more you do something, the better you become at doing it. The adage of practice makes perfect is true.

Teaching is all about the learner and what he/she brings to the learning. Children of poverty do not bring the same experiences to school even if they have similar cultures. The lack of resources leaves students of poverty without the rich learning experiences, health, or peace of mind that like children with basic resources have. The goal for educators must be to "see the world" from their view in order to give the students a new view and understanding of the world. The first step to doing that is to identify the problem of being a child in poverty.

Children of poverty live in situations where there is often a high level of stress and or fear. The stress may be in the form of conflict among family members or in the form of fear for what tomorrow may bring. Since fear can bring anger, many students are angry at their lives and the things that they are lacking.

The teacher is the closest one to the learner (other than parents) and must be the one who initiates the change, provides avenues for success, encourages, and reassures students. As an educator, it's up to the teacher to be sensitive to those who lack resources and struggle mentally, emotionally, socially, or academically. Here are some suggestions:

- Be intentional in noticing those students who come from homes where resources are lacking.
- Strive to first meet the primary needs (clothes and food).

- Seek out all resources available through the school, district, community, state, and federal government need to be made available.
- Check with the school counselor who often has resources that can be helpful.

The key to helping these children is education. The primary instrument is the teacher.

Consequently, what is the role of the teacher? First, the teacher must understand educational neuroscience or at least enough to know that the discoveries and recommendations for learning are accurate and effective. The teacher must be the change agent driven to bring about a change in the brain through actions that can help to rewire the brain and repair damage by "growing the brain." Next, the teacher must be familiar with those approaches to teaching that will be successful for these learners. Finally, the teacher must be an advocate for the learner, supporting and encouraging success that can be achieved. In regard to dealing with students of poverty, the teacher must do several things. Many of these items have been listed as essential practices earlier. Since they are best practices, teaching children of poverty means going beyond the essentials because many of these students have greater needs. Some of those practices include:

- *Develop a learning community within the classroom.* Establish morning sharing or meetings that present concerns and tackle problems jointly to build unity. Use daily language that defines the class as a team with shared visions and goals. Use guidelines from respected character development programs ("Leader in Me") to set the norms for social interaction.
- *Build and maintain a trusting, caring rapport with students.* This is not a quick process. Be consistent and intentional in all interactions, reactions, and choice of words. Provide evidence as often as possible with your support through praise to others and notes to parents with specific accom-

plishments. Build a rapport that depicts genuine care and concern for students.

- *Be an advocate, protector, and supporter* of the learner. Demonstrate that role through daily actions, words, and gestures.
- *Do an interest survey and identify what each child finds interesting.* Develop curriculum that can touch those areas of interest. Individualize as much as possible.
- *Modify the curriculum as needed to meet the needs of the children.* Change the numbers of items assigned at one time as well as the type of work required. Rather than a page of math problems, assign five.
- *Begin and maintain ongoing assessment to determine and support the levels and needs of the students.* Do not limit the assessment to pencil-paper. Include observations, demonstrations, oral explanations/discussions, art, music, and drama as avenues for expression and evidence of knowledge and understanding.
- *Set goals with students,* allowing them input and understanding of "stretching the learning."
- *Celebrate small accomplishments* as well as those larger goals.
- *Teach, discuss, engage in the learning, discuss, review, and reteach in a different way.*
- *Use a spiral type curriculum* or simply spiral back to previously learned concept to internalize the learning, solidify concepts, and to activate a strong or strengthen memory. Expose students to the new learning repeatedly in various ways throughout the year.
- *Use low readability levels with high interest books.*
- *Plan and take field studies.* If funding is not available through the school, solicit help from churches and community leaders. Fundraisers will provide money (such as selling popcorn at recess).
- *Use picture books* explaining that they are "everybody" books and demonstrate their value through regular use.

- *Collect teaching aids that enrich learning* to include manipulates for math, authentic artifacts for history/social studies, supplies for science experiments, and anchor charts that provide visual clues for quick reference and to help in the learning.
- *Plan for success* with each child through level appropriate work. It does not need to be too easy or little effort will be invested. It does not need to be too hard because students will easily become frustrated.
- *Jointly set goals* that are achievement but require effort.
- *Give value to the learning* by making direct connections to real life.
- *Give value to the child* through acknowledging what he might say or do, encouragement, specific feedback, and aid when needed.
- *Model positive attitudes* and a healthy way to approach problems or behaviors.
- *Be specific with directions* and clear with assignments.
- *Explain your thinking process*, particularly when problem solving.
- *Help learners understand that they can increase knowledge and learn.*
- *Make learning achievable* through effective strategies using various modalities and authentic learning activities.
- *Set up an environment* that is conducive to learning with visual, auditory, and kinesthetic. Do an interest survey and identify what each child finds interesting. Develop curriculum that can touch those areas of interest. Individualize as much as possible.
- *Overlearn, reflect, repeat.* Allow students the joy of knowing the answers. Overlearn to build confidence, experience success, and instill a love of learning.
- *Instill in students a mind-growth attitude.* In simple terms, "explain that 'you can grow your brain.'" Deep understanding of how learning can occur invites effort on the part of the learner.

- *With every lesson, be aware of assessing prior knowledge.* New learning must be built upon prior knowledge so connections can be made. Ask questions to make sure the knowledge is there. If it isn't, build knowledge by revisiting foundation skills, understanding, or experience.
- *Scaffold content* areas by bombarding senses with visuals (videos), artifacts (manipulatives), and auditory information. Ensure that the modality used is understood by learners.
- *Provide basic facts for the new learning* through books at a lower reading level to enable easy reading and understanding.
- *Use problem-based learning* to engage the student.
- *Incorporate reflection time* in the lessons to make connections.
- *Help students understand the process and be supportive.* Learning is hard work. Rewiring means establishing new networks in the brain. It can be frustrating and very tiresome.
- *Have short, focused, interactive lessons* that are engaging.
- *Homework must be work that strengthens* the purposed new learning. While some places no longer allow teachers to give homework, if it is permitted the work needs to be at an independent working level of complexity. The assignment is to establish a solid foundation to support new learning.
- *Utilize differentiated instruction* both in the class and outside (homework) to allow students to engage in the learning through various modalities.
- *Use visual learning coupled with auditory explanations* to increase the recall by six times. Scientists have determined that we remember pictures more easily than words. Provide visual clues with each learning experience (Zadina, 2014).
- *Plan for varied perceptions.* We do not all see things the same way. Moreover, is the reality with learners who have deficits because of poverty. Be aware of possible perception differences as a result of cultural and diversity. Training and education can help. Our experiences, biases, worldviews,

and other individual differences make us see the world through varied lens.

- *Engage students in learning through field studies*, either actual field trips or virtual field trips via videos or computer programs. Experiences build learning. Many children of poverty do not have experiences that are common.

- *Identify or develop a program* within the daily routine that provides specific guidelines for what is expected of students with planned outcomes (within reason). These students often do not know the "hidden rules of society." Consequently, they do not understand the results of certain actions. Consider books such as *The Leader in Me, The 7 Habits of Highly Effective People*, or *The 7 Habits of Highly Effective Families* as a resource. If funding is a problem, visit the flea market, thrift shops, or used books on Amazon. The guide is worth the investment.

- *Demonstrate your alliance* through support emotionally, physically, and mentally. Express concerns in words. "I care about you and how you feel." Do not be surprised if the words are perceived as worthless. Many children of poverty find words empty because of previous experiences. Use them anyway but bring them to life with actions.

- *Build a network of safety* for students to take the risk of learning. This network is built on trust and established evidence that no harm will come their way in the form of failure, ridicule, or hopelessness. The teacher is the only one who can build this protection, and it is established through the development of a caring relationship. Caution: the process is painfully slow. Do not give up.

- *Establish ongoing communication with parents* and be their advocate through personal phone calls (periodically) or personal notes. Use the newsletters to celebrate and express appreciation to them for their efforts and support. (See newsletter below.) Make them feel like each parent is special and their children are equally as special. Find out what they need and what the school can do to help them. Make them aware of sources that are available to help. Find out if educational programs can be offered for non- English speaking parents in to improve English, parenting classes, etc. Support them in their struggles.

- *Send goodie notes home* (or a phone call, email, text, etc.) regularly on even the most challenging students at a time when parents least expect them. Make sure the student has something that you can credit him with doing successfully or correctly. (See sample notes in Appendix A.)
- *Make learning fun and exciting.* It is unrealistic to assume every lesson will be another journey into "fun land."

However, there are ways to make each experience more enjoyable. Many times, a teacher will have to "undo" past negative experiences with learning to win over these children. Provide as much active engagement as possible.

- *Develop afterschool reading clubs. American Girls* or *Dear America* are great books that offer a series for girls, and *My Name is America* is a good one for boys.

1. Develop a proposal (see Appendix B).
2. Get one or two (or one faculty member and/or a parent) faculty members to commit to help with each club.
3. Obtain clearance from administration.
4. Determine a date (once a month) and day of the week for the monthly meetings.
5. Try writing grants (within district or state) for money to obtain books, rewards, and food.
6. For each meeting, try to make connections with historical time periods and possibly social studies for that grade level. Each meeting, share books, read, focus on significance of related historical period, have snacks, and for the girls, sharing of dolls (if any have American Girl dolls). At each meeting, girls who read a book, wrote a summary, and placed their names in a box

for a drawing for an American Girl doll. Each time a girl read a book, the name could go into the box. The more books read, the greater the chance to win. The doll was purchased with funds from a sponsor. One was awarded each semester.

7. Develop the same type of club for the boys.

Conclusion

Learners who are living in poverty and lack resources come into the classroom with different prior knowledge, physical concerns, mental abilities, and social/emotional issues. Identifying the needs of these students is the beginning to helping. Establishing a trusting relationship builds a foundation where risk-taking will occur. Strategies that have been proven to be effective with these children who view the world differently must be implemented for success. The approach to teaching and learning is one that focuses on showing the way to learning by explaining thought processes, providing tangibles, presenting information in multiple ways, validating efforts, encouraging risk-taking, and repetition. Students will respond when teachers are trusted, success is reachable, value in learning is established, the learning is authentic and meaningful, and there are celebrations in accomplishments.

Poverty is a condition that can profoundly impact lives. For children growing up in poverty, it begins with stunting the development of various parts of the brain that profoundly impacts on student learning. Children growing in up in poverty have deficits in memory, processing skills, attention spans, social interaction, emotional maturity, and mental aptitude. They are exposed to hunger, poor health, high levels of stress, crime, violence, drugs, and abuse. In addition, poverty puts learners in a situation where they feel hopeless and incapable of learning. Failures and ridicule contribute to low self-esteem and frustration.

A step to applying a cure for this disease-like situation is a force that provides hope, encouragement, and opportunities for success. The teacher is this force. Brain research has identified strategies that can be used to "grow the brain" or help children of poverty to learn. These specific techniques help to rewire the brain in such a way as to understand new concepts and learn. There is help, and changes can be made. The teacher is a change agent in combatting the damage of poverty, but in order to make it happen, *you will need to pray.*

Prayer

Father,

You have selected me to be an instrument of Your work.
Use me now to help these children who have so much to lose.
Help me help them to learn.
Make resources available to meet their primary needs
So that their other needs can be met.
Repair any damage that may have been done through inadequate resources.
Allow them to learn and grow.
Thank You, dear Lord.
Amen.

Something to make you smile

This happened long before the movie, A Christmas Story, was ever produced.

It was a cold morning with temperatures near freezing. The bell for school to begin was close to ringing, and there were only a few children outside the doors. They were slowly wandering into the school building except for a few out by the flagpole.

Mrs. Campbell came walking very quickly toward the office.

"Where's the nurse?" Mrs. Campbell asked with urgency and a hint of panic in her voice.

"She just arrived," the school secretary explained. "I think she's putting her lunch in the lounge."

Before Mrs. Campbell could race into the lounge, Mrs. Moore, the school nurse, came into the office.

"I need help," she began, "Darrin tried to lick the flagpole. Now, he can't move his tongue. It's stuck to the pole!"

Mrs. Moore stood still in unbelief. "Are you trying to be funny?" she asked.

The office secretaries revealed their shock and, at the same time, began to smile in disbelief.

"No, you know Darrin. He's always trying new things. Someone convinced him to do it," Mrs. Campbell explained.

"Okay. Let's get some water."

The rescue was not a pretty sight since Darrin was trying to speak and shout while the nurse poured the water over the pole to release his tongue. Nevertheless, Darrin was free to go and try more new things.

When I saw the movie, A Christmas Story, I thought they got the idea from Darrin.

5

Diversity

"I do things differently. Americans just don't do it the way we did it at home. I'm different. I think different, and I just don't fit in here."

These words ring in my heart as I remember my mother's voice wrought with hurt, frustration, and hopelessness. Momma was a native German. She met Daddy in Heidelberg, Germany, where he was stationed in the US army. One day, he broke his arm and went to the hospital. Momma worked in the army hospital as a switchboard operator. They met, dated, and married.

After serving his time in Germany, they moved to the South Carolina. Several years after living in the United States, Momma got her American citizenship. Her knowledge of American history and geography exceeded that of many native Americans. Despite her relatives in Germany viewing her as being "Americanized" and far more American than German in her actions and thinking, Mamma continued to struggle to "fit in" in America. She felt that others viewed her as inferior because of her background (German), and her slight accent (that I thought was noticeable but not obvious) made it apparent that she was not from South Carolina or anywhere in the United States.

Mamma was fluent in English, extremely smart, and very competent in her work. Since she worked for Americans in Germany, she was around Americans and familiar with not only the language but also the ways of Americans. Nevertheless, Mamma felt the pangs of discrimination because of her heritage. At work, she felt overlooked despite her knowledge, experience, and expertise. Her comment was, "They don't like Germans. I'm different."

I argued with Momma because I did not see a difference. We are the same. It's just your personality that makes you different, and we are all different because we are all individuals. I felt strongly about that and reminded her regularly.

That was my view for years until I taught Sam. Sam was not a native American. His mannerisms were different, his accent was obvious, and his dress was a little different. Sam was not like the other students in the way he acted. Finally, I started to realize that while he was of the same race as me, he was not of the same culture. Social norms were not the same. It went beyond personality and individual differences. Maybe, Momma was right. Then, I began to really consider what she said; cultural differences do make a difference. We are all different.

My own mother tried to convince me that she did not see the world through the same cultural glasses, yet I could not understand. I assumed because we were the same race, in the same country, spoke the same language, and followed the same social rules, we were the same. It took years before I considered the powerful educational implications behind the point that she was trying to make.

Education courses talk about individual differences, various learning styles/modalities, demographics, and (Howard Gardner's theory of) multiple intelligences. These variations alone make it challenging for a teacher to meet the needs of the students in a classroom. How very much greater is that range of differences in a classroom with a widely diverse group of students who represent different cultures, races, backgrounds, demographics, and speak different languages. Meeting the needs of so many different students is a significant problem in education.

Teaching in a diverse society

Today, more than ever before, we have a wide variety of cultures represented in our classrooms. According to the National Center for

Educational Statistics, 9.4 percent of the students in classrooms are ELL (English language learners) students. In some cities, it is as much as 14 percent, and the numbers are growing. This rapid increase in students of different countries has a profound impact on teachers because it is up to the teachers to meet their varied needs.

These students enter our classrooms, sometimes, not knowing the language at all and certainly not understanding the culture or the way things are done. The teacher must be the one to guide the students in a reassuring way to help them overcome the challenges that would be hard for an adult and is much greater for a young child.

Unfortunately, I am confident that there are many teachers who do not see the cultural differences in the ELL (formally called ESOL) students coming into their classrooms and how very difficult it may be for some students. While those very differences serve to make the learning richer for each student in the class, unless the teacher builds a foundation for the respect of all students, those who are "different" will be made to feel so. Moreover, those very differences can build a wall between learning and not learning.

While delighting in what each new culture can bring to the learning, the teacher must make sure all needs are being met. In addition to the many individual differences present in a classroom, students from different cultures present another element of variation.

The teacher has the responsibility of reaching each student, establishing a line of communication with each, and meeting the needs of each student. In addition to using the best basic practices of teaching mentioned earlier, a teacher must try to do the things to make teaching more effective. The first and primary thing to do is to make sure that the classroom is inviting and supportive of every student that is in the room.

Build upon the community of learners. The first day of school, the teacher must establish the members of the class as a community of learners in support of and caring for each other.

The process does not occur overnight. Consistent emphasis on working together for a shared vision and to help each student is built upon the words that are spoken about the class and how the class is viewed by others. When new students arrive, they are immediately accepted into the group because they are in the class and share the common goal of learning and caring for each other.

Research the culture. Find out about the culture from the language to the acceptable social behavior. Some things that are acceptable in our culture (American) is not acceptable in other cultures. Mannerisms and body language are means of communication, but do not communicate the same to all people in all cultures. Find out what is appropriate and what is not. After collecting enough data to begin the understanding, talk with the parents (using an interpreter if needed and available) and ask what is acceptable behavior. Be respectful of what is respected by them and share that with the class to ensure the class responds to the student with respect.

Identify influences of other cultures on our society. Let the students realize that even our language is influenced and made up of contributions from other languages. Some of our traditions, foods, and customs are taken from other countries. Help students understand that our country is richer for the influence of other countries on our lives.

Provide multicultural books. Encourage students to find out about other cultures, identifying the ways they are alike and different from their own.

Celebrate cultures. Take the time to invite all students to research their heritage and share what they learn. Let everyone know that each person is valued and appreciated.

Invite the parents to the class. What an enriching lesson to be shared with natives from another country sharing their culture with the students. It's authentic and can be very interesting. The more the parents can bring to share, the better (food, clothing, money, or items of special meaning or interest). In their sharing, students can gain knowledge about another culture while learning more about their own classmate.

Be inclusive. Celebrations of holidays need to include respect for the way the new family does things and celebrates holidays. For example, Christmas trees may be done differently or not used at all. Make accommodations to show respect for their views. Sharing during events at school, make sure the family is included with an invitation to share what they want to share. At Christmas, traditions and explanations for the way things are done is a lesson in and of itself.

Be sensitive. Sometimes, common actions can be offensive or hurtful to those of another culture. Noticing how students react to all situations can be informative of how they feel. A watchful eye and loving heart can note subtle hurts that can leave scars. Being sensitive is the beginning to repairing any unintentional hurts.

Research linguistic traits. Identify the linguistic traits of the students with different languages. Use that information to guide your instruction with the student. Learn how second language may impact on literacy.

Collaborate with other professionals. Seek assistance and understanding from the ELL (English language learners) teacher to help you with language, cultural, and social differences.

Provide accommodations. Students new to our country and unfamiliar with our language will need extra help. Most schools have an ELL teacher available. If not, sometimes, other teachers who can help assist the student to make the adjustment and learn the language.

Children are amazing in that they can sometimes communicate with each other despite a language barrier. Assign a study buddy to help the new student with routines and adjustments.

Teaching accommodates begin with a formal or informal assessment. The new student's ability to understand the language is pivotal to the next steps. If the student has an adequate level of understanding of the language, then in addition to some of the essential practices, a teacher can do the following:

- *Include the student in more group work.* Children learn from other children quickly. Engagement is still a primary effective teaching strategy. In a group setting, there is not as great a threat for failure. Instead, other children love to help each other, and the students will happily "show" and "teach" someone how to do something.
- *Make instruction very visual.* Good practices encourage teachers to "bombard" students with information from all modalities. This practice is critical for ELL students.

- *Seek out the ELL teacher.* Ask the ELL teacher for assistance. Maintain ongoing communication to enrich the activities that you plan and to make sure that you are on the best track for optimum results in learning for the student.
- *Pre-teach the ELL student to give him a "head start."* Allowing the student to know in advance the new material may relieve a level of stress and allow both the ELL teacher and the student to prepare before the lesson.
- *Allow for an adjustment period.* Initially, the student may be hesitant, reserved, or terribly intimidated and frightened. If, at first, he is not responding or participating, let him get to a comfortable level before encouraging him to become more active.
- *Help the student to know that mistakes are understandable.* Make it clear that he will not be thought less for the mistakes. Have the other children try his language and let him see that it is difficult. Teach him how to not take himself seriously.
- *Learn about the culture of the student.* Let him know you know and are impressed with your new learning.
- *Let the student shine as an authority of his culture.* Encourage the student to share pertinent and interesting facts with the class.

If the student does not understand the language, then, the approach must be a little different with many more visual aids and a lot more help from the ELL teacher.

Assessing ELL students

Teachers can design informal assessments and maintain anecdotal records to document progress and drive instruction for ELL students. Assessments that require demonstration of content knowledge is effective and particularly appropriate for experiments in science and math calculations. Group or choral responses can provide information about understanding without embarrassment or intimidation for the student. For example: hand signals, response cards (boards), or four corners. (Students move to a corner that represents their response to the prompt. The choices include strongly agree, strongly disagree, agree somewhat, and not sure.) Choral readings can provide practice through support of other children.

Unfortunately, some states require all students to participate in the standardized testing programs. If that is the case for your students, I encourage you to talk with the student and make sure it is understood that the results of the test are not critical but rather more practice. It is sad to think a student must take a test when he/she cannot read the test or understand the language.

Conclusion

Unless you are of native-American decent, you or your family are immigrants to this country. It may have been hundreds of years ago or within the last century or decade. What we have brought to this country in shared traditions and cultures has made our country what it is. Each person has a rich background that must be honored and appreciated. The teacher's attitude and appreciation for all types of people and cultures will be seen and picked up by students. The teacher is always the role model, the leader, and the "trendsetter" for how students will respond to any change.

The goal of the teacher is to help the new student be received, respected, and appreciated into the community of learners. The greater the difference, the greater the opportunity for the teacher to demonstrate how to accommodate, accept, and value someone who is from another country or culture. When the teacher opens the classroom with genuine love and compassion, the students will do the same. In order to this to happen, *you will need to pray*.

Prayer

Father,

Help me to treat others the way I want to be treated.
Let the love You show me be what I show to others.

Grant me understanding and wisdom to embrace
and appreciate all others.
Let me be a role model for these students, as
Christ is a role model for me.
Amen.

Something to make you smile

To make students more aware of their heritage, improve their self-concepts, and have them take pride in where they were from, I asked the children to research their backgrounds. After explaining how we all (through parents or past relatives) came to this country from other countries (unless we are native Americans), I gave myself as an example.

"My mother is from Germany. I was born in Germany, and my daddy is an American. Daddy's family came here from Scotland many, many years ago (1600s). There are so many things that both great Germans and great Scottish people have done that makes me proud of my heritage.

"Boys and girls, I want you to go home and ask your parents about your heritage and where you are from."

Tom's hand went up quickly. "I already know that! I'm from Columbia, and so is my mom and dad."

6

Through the Eyes of a Child

"Get up, Emma! It's time for school," screamed Momma. "It's late. You need to leave."

My head hurt, and it was hard to try to wake up. Last night was another night of Momma and Daddy fighting. Daddy was drunk again. He wanted to listen to his music. It was too loud. Momma tried to make him stop. He shouted bad words at her. She tried to hit him. They fought with each other. Daddy grabbed Momma by the hair and pushed her head against the wall. She screamed. I cried. I cried hard.

Poverty does not cause a man to drink alcohol and become violent with his family. Frustration because of an unhappy family life, a lack of necessities, and too many unpaid bills may cause a man to resort to drugs or alcohol to find some type of solace or escape from a reality that appears overwhelming. The focus is on Emma. What does Emma see? What effect does a night of shouting, fighting, and violence leave on Emma? How does this type of situation influence Emma as she enters the classroom?

Emma is a quiet seven-year-old. She is clean, neat, and polite. Her life consists of school, Momma, Daddy, and their three dogs. The highlights are going to Granny's. Granny gives her candy, buys her clothes, sends her lunch money, and has lots of food, even fruit. But Granny lives eighty miles away, and Emma doesn't get to see her very often.

Right now, Emma must leave for school. She has a mixture of feelings. When she comes into her classroom, those feelings will begin to be revealed despite her efforts to hide them.

Emma is physically tired because of a lack of sleep. There is a heavy feeling and a sadness that cannot be explained. Her sluggishness makes it hard for her to think. She enters the classroom and prepares for the day. Her mind wanders back to Momma. *Is Momma okay? Will Daddy be there when I get home? Will he be drunk? Will someone come and take me to their house for a while? I don't want to go away again. I miss Momma and Daddy. I miss the dogs.*

Her thoughts are interrupted as the teacher calls on her to go to the board. Emma is asked to do a long division problem. Embarrassment and fear overwhelm her. She just stands at the board, unable to speak and certainly unable to do the problem. Her teacher, Mrs. Baker, appears cross and walks over to her. The pang of the ruler both stunts Emma and deeply humiliates her. She has never been punished at school. Emma always follows the rules and shows respect. Slowly, Emma returns to her seat. It was a hard night, and now, it's a very hard day.

What can Mrs. Baker do to help Emma?

Most teachers know their students well. But the busyness of the day can cause teachers to overlook minor symptoms that reflect a problem. This is not the first time that Emma has experienced a difficult night. Frequently occurring behaviors are not considered out of the ordinary. For Emma, it's just another time that Daddy got drunk.

The most difficult task for a teacher is to make time to really connect with students each day. When teachers do that, subtle changes are noted, and steps can be taken to help students like Emma.

Help cannot be given until it is perceived that help is needed. There are things that a teacher can do to help students like Emma. Mrs. Baker (all teachers) need to:

- *Pay attention to each individual student. Establish and maintain a trusting relationship.*

Mrs. Baker walked over to Emma's desk while the other children were busy with their work.

"Good morning, Emma," Mrs. Baker began, "how are you today?"

Emma's response was slow and reflective of uncertainty on what to say. "I'm okay."

"I wondered if you are feeling well," Mrs. Baker continued, "because you look a little tired."

"I didn't sleep much last night. Daddy and Momma were fighting," Emma went on to explain.

Before any help will be received, Mrs. Baker must have already in place a firm relationship built on trust. Otherwise, any efforts on the part of Mrs. Baker will not be received. For Emma, there are many people and things that seem like one thing and turn out to be another. Children are very perceptive, particularly those who have been in untrusting relationships with one or more primary caregivers. They know when teachers (people) genuinely care and want to help. They know when people are just talking with no real concern, and they know they are not to tell others too much information. Trust is important if a teacher wants to get past meaningless talk and gestures that close doors to receiving any help.

- *Take time to comfort and listen.*

    Mrs. Baker began, "Emma, would you like to go to the library for a good book? There is a special place where you can read your book so that others will not bother you. Tell Mrs. Jones that I sent you. When you return, we will go over the work that you missed. We will get you all caught up."

- *Have a system in place to offer the child rest, food (if needed), and time to get back on track of school and learning.*

    "Emma, if you would rather, you know, Mrs. Carney (guidance counselor) said she needed a helper today. I told her I would select a friend to help her. Would you like to do that?" Mrs. Baker offered.

- *Plan for one-on-one instruction and any other accommodations that may be necessary to meet the needs of the student.*

"Emma, there are few things that we went over while you were out of the room. Let's go over these now. I know you can do this if we work together."

- *Be sensitive to each individual child and the reaction he/she will have to actions. Notice changes in behavior.*

When Emma obviously did not understand how to do the long division problem, Mrs. Baker might have realized something is different, since Emma is usually a good student. Here's an approach Mrs. Baker could have used:

When Emma makes no attempt at solving the problem Mrs. Baker might have said, *"Emma, let's do this together. What do you think we do first? It's okay if you don't remember, we can figure this out as a team."*

Or Mrs. Baker could have tried this:

"Emma, pick a friend to help you. Boys and girls, is there someone who can be a helper to Emma today? If so, come on up and do the problem with her."

Being able to "read" children is a talent or skill that must be refined through practice. There are children who would not have been significantly impacted by not knowing how to do the problem at the board. Other children might be dramatized. Teachers need to have a good idea of the reaction of children prior to the action by the teacher. Knowing students is part of the responsibility of teachers.

* * * * *

"Anna, are you dressed and ready to go?"

"But I haven't eaten."

"It's too late. We don't have nothing for you to eat anyway."

Anna looked forward to going to school. It was calmer there. No one bothered her. Her teacher was nice, and the lunch was good.

Anna's family lacked basic resources. Her tattered clothes and free-lunch status confirmed that her family had little money. Many days, she was absent or late arriving at school. Homework was usually incomplete or not attempted.

Despite her shabby clothes, Anna was a cute little girl. Her face revealed sadness and fear. Her soft brown hair gently shaped her tired face. Even with her puffy eyes and drawn face, Anna was pretty. Her teachers said she was always eager to please. She wanted her teacher to like her.

Anna is a little girl who had a home but sometimes lacked basic needs (food, warmth, stability, security, and peace). She sometimes had to live with relatives because there was no heat or lights. Her story is one that focuses on the stresses, fear, uncertainty, and chaos that was part of her daily life.

* * * * *

"It [the shower water] is freezing. The hot water shut off because we didn't pay the bill."

"Seeing a flat screen TV reminds me of things we had before we got poor."

"My dad got laid off. You have to pay the bill, or you get thrown out on the street. We had to leave. I lost my favorite teddy bear in storage."

"We don't get three meals a day. When I feel hungry, I feel weak. I try to think of something else. Sometimes, we have cereal and no milk. Sometimes, I see a cooking show on TV and get hungry."

"We [Kaylie and her friend] like to go canning to make money. Non-squished cans you get five cents. Squished cans two cents."

"We can't afford to pay our bills. I'm afraid we'll be homeless. Me and my brother will starve."

"We are in the homeless shelter. We had a fancy house and flat screen TV. My parents didn't have the money to pay for the house because my dad lost his job. He works at a factory [two hours away]. The rules at the shelter say kids can't stay alone, so we have to ride there with him. Mom brings us back, and then, we go again to pick him up. I watch people walk into their house when we are driving. I wish we had a house to live in."

"I became pregnant at sixteen... On the one hand, my boyfriend was a drug-selling cheater, and on the other hand, I was an unexperienced, premature, and mixed-up drug user with a premature baby."

"I was born into a family that was already in captivity and didn't know how to show me my way out. It is fair to say that my family was one of much dysfunctions and no direction" (Cook 2015).

Heather's situation was one where the lacking element was primarily love and support. While her parents may have "loved" her in a way that she could understand, because they did not know how to express their love in a healthy way.

Poverty has many faces. It is not just the absence of basic needs with all the problems that it brings. Poverty is a situation that makes its victims vulnerable to other conditions. It does not mean that people in poverty will take on these conditions. It means that statistics indicate people in poverty are at a greater risk. Some of those conditions are: (1) violence, (2)drugs, (3) promiscuity, (4) depression, (5) stress, (6) suicide, (7) poor health, (8) incest, (9) theft, (10) antisocial behaviors, (11) emotional disorders, (12) mental disorders, (13) fear, (14) lack of education, and (15) abuse.

Sometimes, it is difficult to identify which condition was present first. If poverty is present, one or more of the other conditions might be near. Poverty can promote, aggravate, or bring on some or all the other conditions.

Because the teacher is sometimes the only stability in the life of children, often, they look forward to coming to school. These two students did not. A good educator is consistent, respectful, and caring. These qualities are not always what is present at home for these children. Encouraging words and positive statements are sounds that resonate in the brain and heart of children who do not regularly hear those sounds. Since the teacher is often a welcomed sight, the teacher is the one to help Cindy and Nathan as well as children like her find hope, love, and success. Otherwise, those elements might be illusive for them. The role of the teacher is:

- model appropriate social behaviors and emotional reactions;
- convey optimism through actions and words, "We can do this together" or "You will get it;"
- establish and maintain ongoing communication with parents;

- be intentional about conveying positive behaviors and achievements to the parents;
- find a modality that will allow expression (writing, art, or music);
- encourage journaling, drawing, or painting to vent and express thoughts;
- plan for successes for children;
- communicate positive behaviors and academic successes to parents;
- talk highly of them in front of other people;
- let them know of their potential and goodness;
- expose them to new experiences through field trips, videos, and books (Nathan does not need this so much, but Cindy does);
- help them make connections with a world that is inviting;
- teach them how to respond to disappointments and when things do not go the way they had planned; and let them see the confidence that you have in their success;

Action steps are built upon individual needs of students. Find out as much as possible about the student(s). Use informal assessments, formal assessments, interest inventories, conferences (with parents and the student), and anecdotal notes based on observations to assess and determine the needs of students. Keep in mind, while there may be similarities between children of poverty (particularly with their needs), each student is different. The impact of very similar situations can leave a very different scar on individual students. Some steps include:

- Establish and maintain a high level of trust through a good rapport with the student. Talk with the student through conference, set him/her up for success during shared times, provide a special task that he/she alone is responsible. Make him/her feel special in an outstanding, positive way.
- Talk with the school counselor about including the child or children in a specific group offered by the counselor that matches the need.

- Establish a good rapport with the parents through continuous correspondence that is positive and encouraging. Send home notes that convey daily or weekly progress with an emphasis on success and achievements.
- Bring hope, peace, and joy to the classroom with smiles, laughter, and positivity.
- Determine the strong modality for learning and for expressing new learning. Utilize that modality as much as possible for assessment (there are several options for modality testing online).
- Encourage journaling, drawing (art), or music as forms of expression.
- Use multiple forms of communication for assignments and any vital information. Anchor charts to reinforce skills or new learning. Assignment boards with repetition verbally.
- Clearly explain the value in specific learning and make a connection with today and the future for that student.
- Do not assume prior knowledge. Assess informally in a nonthreatening or embarrassing way. Explain reasons for everything.
- Provide security. Routines are a form of security. Avoid variations in routine. When the routines are varied, provide support, reassurance, and explanations for why the change is occurring.
- Make sure physical needs are met. In cold weather, seek coats through churches, school counselor, etc. Provide those needed items indirectly and discretely.
- Celebrate achievements both large and small. Provide food (healthy) when possible.
- Be an advocate for the student. Do not hide your support. Share with the class the special connections as we work together toward the common goal of learning and helping each other grow. Stress how we are there for each other.

Is poverty the only culprit keeping some students from learning?

"Mrs. Hawkins, can Nathan stay in your classroom for a while? He's having a hard day," Mrs. Pidel said in a stern voice, reflecting both aggravation and annoyance.

"Sure, come on in, Nathan. Have a seat over here. Tell me about your day," I said in a matter-of-fact way.

"Mrs. Pidel is just picking on me. I didn't do anything. Josh was making faces at me. I just told him to stop," Nathan began.

"You didn't touch him, did you?" I said in an assuring yet verifying way.

"Not really. I just tried to get him out of my way," Nathan explained.

"Did Josh get upset?" I asked, trying to make a point.

"He's such a baby. He acted like he was hurt, but I hardly touched him. I should have hit him hard if he is going to get me in trouble anyway!" Nathan shouted.

"Calm down. We can figure this out. You know, I care about you and do not want you to get in trouble. We'll come back to this. Tell me about your day before this happened." I wanted to see if he had other altercations today.

"It's been a bad day..." Nathan continued to explain.

Nathan frequently has difficulty that erupts into physical confrontations. While he does not lack for anything materially, Nathan struggles with others. He is an only child and is accustomed to having his way. His parents are supportive, but nothing has altered his actions or his reactions to others. He goes on trips with his parents to neighboring states, yet he seems to get upset with others very quickly. Nathan consistently does things that must be addressed because he hurts other children or is extremely disrespectful to teachers. Despite his age (third grader), he backs down to no one. Those bigger or older receive the same aggression as those smaller and younger. Nathan's been suspended several times, but nothing seems to make a difference. He has potential, but he's too busy getting in trouble to learn. Nathan expects what he wants when he wants it and in the manner he wants it. Nathan needs help.

* * * * *

"I'm not doing this junk! I don't have to, and I don't want to," Cindy began as soon as she entered the classroom.

"Good morning, Cindy," I said with a smile. *"How are you today?"*

"Terrible! Terrible! I hate school, and I hate Mrs. Jordan. She's stupid!" Cindy's loud shouting startled those around and caused them to stop what they were doing to see how the disruption would be addressed. All eyes were on me to see what I would do.

Cindy walked over to a desk and slammed her hand down!

The other students jumped.

"Cindy, take some quiet time. Come, sit over here where no one can bother you. When you want to talk with me, let me know. I am here, and I care about you," I spoke so softly the words were almost like a whisper. As I spoke, I tried to make eye contact with Cindy so that I might provide some reassurance.

Cindy's explosions in class are not uncommon. They happen almost every day. She's very frustrated with school and appears to be frustrated with everyone in her life. Her home life is not great, but she is not lacking food, clothes, and basic care. Cindy struggles academically because of great "gaps" in her learning. She has little patience with herself or others. As a third grader, she's had a while to be retold the inabilities and inadequacies that she has.

In Cindy's eyes, she has no self-worth. She receives mixed messages at home, depending on the state of her parents and which one interacts with her, but most of the time, the comments are negative. Her emotional outbursts and aggressive behaviors have made other children avoid and dislike her. The behavior problems have taken her away from learning opportunities. Cindy needs some type of help.

The rest of the story

Nathan's parents continued to try to work with the school. Eventually, Nathan was a regular visitor with those visits becoming a reward for good behavior and effort in the classroom. His potential became more obvious as his grades improved. Nathan started to get along better with other students which lead him to participation in sports. He excelled in this area.

With time, Cindy began to trust my genuine concern for her and her well-being. I was able to show her that she could learn, and she did make academic and social progress. She had a long way to go, but she was on the right road.

These situations represent just a few of the many challenging situations with children who are not learning. But these students are not lacking food, shelter, clothes, or basic care. They are lacking fundamental emotional needs. In some cases, they are lacking consistency with discipline, and in other cases, they are lacking love. These children look at life as if there are people who do not like them, and there are.

Helping students have a different view of the world is a challenge for teachers. It can be accomplished when students are exposed to new learning, new caring, and new accomplishments. When teachers help students see what they can do, what is available, and that things can be different, then a change can occur. Teachers are the key to showing children a different type of world.

The same strategies used to help children lacking food, shelter, clothing, etc. can be used to help children like Nathan and Cindy. Children who are lacking view of the world through different lens. Sometimes, they feel slighted and that life is hard and unfair. The teacher is one who can show the way to see a brighter tomorrow through care, success, and guidance today. Here are the key approaches that can make a difference:

- Establish and maintain a high level of trust through a good rapport with the student.
- Be a role model.
- Be positive yet realistic in goals.
- Send home goodie notes.
- Determine their strengths. Determine the strong modality for learning and for expressing new learning. Utilize that modality as much as possible for assessment.
- Encourage expression. The anger must be released. Find a modality that will allow expression (writing, art, or music).

Encourage journaling, drawing, or painting to vent and express thoughts.

- Teach them how to appropriately respond to disappointments and when things do not go the way they had planned.
- Let them see the confidence that you have in their achieving success.
- Celebrate achievements, both large and small.
- Be an advocate for the student.
- Talk with the school counselor about including the child or children in a specific group offered by the counselor that matches the need.
- Bring hope, peace, and joy to the classroom with smiles, laughter, and positivity.

The older the child, the harder it will be to change the way they see themselves and the world. Changes take time and are only effective when there is continuity. Routines are security for children. Establish good routines that are fun and exciting. Make daily events and happenings spectacular. Plan for success and let them know you expect it from them.

Conclusion

While we cannot really see the world through the eyes of children of poverty, perhaps, a glimpse is enough to stimulate action. The reality is unless we have lived it by doing without what we take for granted (food, shelter, clothes, self-respect), felt it, the fear, pain, and hopelessness, we cannot appreciate the unbelievable difficulties and endless cycle of poverty. The cycle can be broken. It begins with caring people who are determined to make a significant difference and are willing to deal with the angry students, discouraged parents, indifferent officials, and "blind" state departments who cannot see beyond achievement and test scores.

Through the eyes of many children, life doesn't make sense. What is obviously wrong or inappropriate and inexcusable is normal for these children. Life is hard, hurting, and hopeless for many. It appears very unfair and harsh, devoid of hope, and full of unsurmountable obstacles. It's not just those who deal with poverty, meaning they lack food, water, shelter, and clothes. Other students have food, shelter, clothes, and basic care, but they lack emotional support, understanding of appropriate social interactions, and unconditional love.

For some students, lacking and wanting is part of the daily routine. Moving from place to place is a lifestyle and being in areas of violence is just what happens. Fear, hunger, and pain are sometimes "too close for comfort."

Trying to help these children begins by helping them see the hope and reality of living in an environment of safety, security, and well-being where necessities are available and being happy is normal. There are people who care. There are programs to help. The challenge is to connect the people who care and the programs that help with the children who need the assistance.

With great teachers, school offers food, consistent routines, and a level of physical comfort. The teacher is the link to provide some hope, help, and a new view of the world. When care, support, continuity, and new learning are part of the everyday experience at school, then hope can join, and the child will see the world through different eyes. To make it happen, *you will need to pray.*

Prayer

> Lord God,
>
> Provide a way to show the world to these children
>   in such a way
> As to give them hope.
> Let Your love flow through me and into them.
> Grant me wisdom to deal with each child and the
>   special needs they have.
> Guide me to guide them to a new beginning.
> Amen.

Something to make you smile

"Hello, is this Mrs. Marsh? This is Mrs. Hawkins, I'm calling about Clara," I began.

"What has she done now? That child doesn't know how to behave. She is always getting in trouble. I've done the best that I can. She just won't listen and doesn't care. I really do not know what I am going to do with her," Mrs. Marsh spoke so fast and without taking a breath that I could not start to explain why I had called. Finally, she stopped.

"I just wanted to let you know that Clara helped another student today with her math. Her assistance was not only appreciated by me, but the other student was happy to have her help. Clara is a joy to teach. I just wanted to let you know." My words were spoken with sincere gratitude and amazement.

There was a long silence. It was as if Mrs. Marsh had never heard anything good about Clara.

Then, I heard her respond. "Oh!" Mrs. Marsh began. "A teacher has never called to say something good about Clara. Are you sure you are talking about my child?"

7

Teaching in a Changing Society

It is change, continuing change, inevitable change,
that is the dominant factor in society today. No sensible
decision can be made any longer without considering not
only the world as it is, but the world as it will be.

—Isaac Asimov

Approximately twenty-five years ago, in a professional development seminar, the speaker explained that one day soon, teachers would no longer be considered the primary source of information in the classroom. Instead, they would be facilitators. Information would be readily accessible, and teachers would need to teach student how to access that information and how to determine what information is valuable or accurate. The speaker was correct. Technology allows information to be a "Google" away. The role of the teacher has changed.

* * * * *

Many years ago, Mrs. Coles was my fifth-grade teacher. One of the things that I loved about her class was the book she read to us after lunch. She was talented with her reading in that she read with expression and passion. Of course, I cried when she read Old Yeller. Also, she read us a devotional daily, and then, we said the pledge. Mrs. Coles told us what to do and when to do it, and she was always right. There were never arguments. Our teacher was the leader in our class; the one who held all knowledge, the one highly respected by both students and parents, and the one who drank a Coke and ate crackers at recess.

I do not remember Mrs. Coles having to deal with any discipline problem except for Tracey. Tracey was not disrespectful; she was just Tracey. Since I was a shy, withdrawn child and Tracey was the opposite, she was difficult to ignore. Perhaps, her fiery-red hair pulled back in the typical ponytail made her even more noticeable. Tracey was not like other students in her behavior. She was talkative with a high energy level and could not be still, even for a few minutes. Despite her high activity level, she was in what was known at that time as "the top class." Tracey was smart.

Mrs. Coles did not have other students behaving anywhere like Tracey. It was apparent that she had difficulty responding to the "unusual" behavior of Tracey. Perhaps, Mrs. Coles thought Tracey could control herself better. One day, it was obvious that the teacher was at her "wits' end" with the student. Mrs. Coles's response was one that was not questioned at that time, and while being a disciplinarian was a role of the teacher, she handled things in a different way than the way it would be handled today.

"Sit down!" Mrs. Coles shouted. "If you don't stop talking and moving around, I'll tape your mouth shut and tie you down in a chair."

Tracey's blue eyes almost twinkled when she spoke, "I was just helping Martha. She dropped her pencil, and I picked it up."

"I am in the middle of a lesson!" Mrs. Coles continued. "You're not to get out of your seat when I'm teaching! You know that!"

Tracey appeared undaunted as she almost skipped over to her seat, her red ponytail hair bouncing with each step.

Mrs. Coles's frustration with Tracey could be seen on her face and in her tone. She went over to her desk where she found some tape and rope. With both items in one hand, Mrs. Coles used her other hand to pull a chair to the front of the room.

"Come up here, Tracey," Mrs. Coles sternly commanded.

Tracey hopped up and plopped down into the chair. Mrs. Coles began to place tape over Tracey's mouth and then begin to tie her hands together.

"There, don't move." Mrs. Coles sighed as if relieved. Almost imme-diately, a smile took over the teacher's face as she watched Tracey in amazement. As if it were just another talent, Tracey began to wiggle out of the ropes, then out of the tape. Her arms and legs wildly moving as she laughter. The class began to laugh as Mrs. Coles looked on in amazement to see that Tracey had managed to wiggle out of the binding twine and freed herself of the tape.

This would not happen today. The times have changed. The role of the teacher is still the one that must address disciplinary issues, but today, most schools have a specific person who handles situations that exceed minor problems. That person may be a behavior coach, assistant principal, or principal.

A teacher today has the knowledge to know that Tracey cannot control her actions. The rope and tape would not have been consid-ered as an option. A good teacher would recognize the symptoms and seek help from parents and other professionals. Tracey would be given help and an opportunity to learn, and it would occur in a respectful manner. In the schools today, a teacher must be a "diag-nostician" for behavioral and learning difficulties. The teacher is not necessarily expected to solve all problems, but she/he is expected to contact those who can.

Many things have changed in education. Most of the changes have been beneficial to the students and have enhanced learning. The changes have been in practices, policies, procedures, pupils, parents' involvement, and pedagogy, as well as a change in the role of the teacher.

The role of the teacher has changed

Teaching has always been a noble profession. However, it was once thought of as a "glorified babysitting position." The teachers spoke with authority and were looked upon as one with knowledge, but many really thought anybody can teach children. The respect is still there but in a different way. Teachers are questioned. They must maintain moral standing that exceeds that of others, but there are things that have changed.

The teacher must be able to identify any problem that prohibits a student from learning. Then, the teacher must either eliminate the problem or call in other professionals who can. This is just one of the many roles of the teacher in today's classroom. Here are some more:

- researcher
- lifelong learner
- leader
- mentor
- role model
- learning program designer
- manager
- counselor
- liaison between the school and parents/community
- diagnostician for learning problems
- technology specialist
- disciplinarian

Poor Mrs. Coles had many responsibilities and with much less knowledge and understanding of how children learn or behave than teachers of today. But she did have autonomy. She could run her classroom as she felt appropriate. Her curriculum was flexible if she talked about some of the items in the textbooks. Her approach to learning was her choice. The time invested in daily subjects was up to her. Mrs. Coles oversaw her students, her class, and her routine. This occurred over fifty years ago.

In a classroom twenty-five years ago, things would be different. However, some things would not have changed. The teacher would be able to determine variations in the curriculum.

* * * * *

While studying Egypt in social studies, my fourth-grade students became intrigued with the process of mummification. The entire fourth-grade class appeared to have an insatiable appetite for more information about Egypt, the geography, the people, the customs, and the cultural. It seemed only logical to allow the students to lead the way in the learning. So, we took a week to explore as much as possible about Egypt. This happened about twenty-five years ago before policy dictated the curriculum and how long to stay on one topic. Teachers had autonomy and input to the decisions made about curriculum and what happened in the classroom.

The students made informational books, maps, and of course, did extensive research on Egypt. The pyramids as well as human anatomy in relation to the mummification process became a focus of study. Papier-mache was used to make a "body." Spaghetti was placed in the head to serve as brains. Jell-O was placed in the chest cavity for the heart. Other organs were represented with food items. The most fascinating part of the activity was when the students used a "hook" (knitting needle) to extract the "brain.

The students were engaged, excited, and eager to find out more about Egypt. This was one of the best lessons I remember teaching/leading.

* * * * *

Beginning in the year 2000, the superintendent of our district was insightful enough to realize that the students entering the elementary schools would need more than what those graduating from the high schools at that time had received in preparation for the future. Just as what the students of the 19th century had in school adequately met their needs; but that same curriculum and format is vastly lacking for the 20th-century students. The goal of the teachers must be to prepare students for the 21st century. Many of the goals from the 20th century would be outdated and leave students significantly unprepared in a competitive technology-centered world. For this reason, one significant change is in the curriculum.

Would this happen today? Probably not because each subject has a certain content area to be taught within a designated time frame. Going beyond the allocated time would mean something would be omitted. That is not acceptable. Teachers no longer have control over the curriculum. The autonomy of teachers changed. When did the drastic change occur? Two significant actions were catalysts; the report by President Reagan, *A Nation at Risk*, and advances in technology.

The curriculum has changed

In 1983, President Ronald Reagan released a report, *A Nation at Risk*. The report took aim at the schools in our country in condemning them for not keep up with the schools in other leading countries. The results of this action brought about significant changes (Akhtar, 2019):

- Standardized teaching (same curriculum, similar pace). No more teacher autonomy with curriculum.
- Academic standards. All children need to learn the same thing.
- National Board for Professional Teaching Standards. Teachers must have a certain level of competency to teach.
- Technology in the classroom. Integration of technology as an integral part of teaching.
- Smart board replacement of blackboards.

In today's classroom, the curriculum is predetermined and somewhat planned. A long- and short-range planning guide is provided. Often, a curriculum map is given, and teachers are expected to abide by the dates posted on these documents with little or no exceptions to the rule. Teachers do not have the freedom to decide what to teach or when to teach. Standardization of testing, curriculum, and practices take the authority from teachers about most major issues concerning curriculum in the classroom.

More continuity in what is being taught to students is the result of this action. For example, Darrin transferred from one school to another within the district. Unfortunately, the area of study that we were beginning had just been completed at the other school he attended, but the one we had just finished had not been taught. Darrin would miss an entire unit of study despite his living in the same district. This is one reason for the change. Another reason was, of course, test scores. More unity in the course of study was to provide a greater likelihood of higher test scores because all the students were taught the same thing.

The focus of the curriculum for today's students must include skills that promote technology as a fundamental tool for communication and as a method for obtaining new information. The basic curriculum is dominant at the elementary with technology integrated to make the learning more enjoyable and efficient. Variations and innovations are incorporated to keep the information on the "cutting edge." Understanding our history and our past mistakes will always help future generations avoid those same pitfalls. Consequently, the "meat" of the matter will remain. The "side dishes" will change as publishers decide new and more creative ways for teachers to teach the content areas. However, facts and figures are always a "button away." "Siri" and "Alexa" can provide facts from the past and trivia from the present.

The crucial skills that students require are those that stress critical thinking, effective collaboration to maximize achievement, and extraordinary communication skills. Below are more skills and/or character traits that are vital in preparing students for tomorrow:

- *Effective communication.* Students must be proficient in both oral and written communication. Listening and public speaking are equally as important. Our world is becoming "smaller." We can Skype, FaceTime, text, call, or visit most places in the world within a few minutes to hours.
- *Collaboration.* Working effectively with others having shared goals is at the heart of utilizing maximum resources. Students must learn the process of working with others in such a way as to have a unanimous commitment, united efforts, and a genuine understanding of what each person can offer as to obtain the desired results. To achieve this, there must be a strong skill set for cooperation and teamwork.
- *Leadership.* Students must understand the qualities of an outstanding leader. Having opportunities to assume a leadership role is the beginning to teaching students the skills and responsibilities involved.

- *Critical thinking, analysis, and evaluation.* Students must be able to think critically, figure out alternative solutions, synthesize, analysis, and evaluate. Superficial or surface-level thoughts will not meet the needs of tomorrow's world of technology and fast-paced living. "Thinking out of the box" must become a part of the routine option in looking for other ways to accomplish goals or complete a task.
- *Problem-solving.* Overcoming obstacles is part of real life living. Students must be prepared to tackle problems, solve them, and move on.
- *Perseverance.* The desire to keep going and trying is a learned skill for many. Most goals require continuous effort and a high level of determination to achieve the goal.
- *Self-discipline.* Learning how to control oneself and the value of delayed gratification is a stepping stone to success. Waiting is not something many of us do well. Only with self-discipline can one maintain despite no evidence of success on the journey to success.
- *Planning.* Looking ahead with intent and tangible plans is how success is attained. Planning is a skill that must be taught.
- *Adaptability/acceptance of change.* More so than perhaps in the past, students will see their worlds changing at a rapid rate. Being able to adapt, modify routes, and move on is imperative for survival.
- *Multiculturalism.* Our world is "smaller." We must teach children how to respect and appreciate differences.
- Help students see the value of looking at things through different cultural "glasses."
- *Global awareness.* Students must learn our place in the world and our responsibility to self and others within our world. Student must learn to value, preserve, and appreciate our Earth and all living creatures on it.
- *Financial literacy.* Understanding the basics of how our financial system works is important for students. General knowledge of saving, spending, and owing will help many

students handle their money more wisely. The elementary school level is not too early to learn this skill.

- *Environmental and conservation literacy.* Part of our changing world includes a changing environment. Teaching students the importance of taking care of what we have begins at a personal level and extends to our Earth. The future is at stake.
- *Health awareness.* Students must realize that our society is dealing with an obesity problem. Being selective with taking care of one's body means proper diet and exercise.

Many of these are character development qualities. In the past, it was primarily the responsibility of parents to instill morals, strong character, and respect for others. Today, that responsibility has been passed on to the school. Many parents still strive to teach their children these traits. The school now includes it in the curriculum.

Teaching practices have changed

"It's time for reading. I need all the Red Birds to come up to the circle," Mrs. Butler announced. "Bring your Think-and-Do Books."

My heart sank. I hated reading, and most of all, I hated Think-and-Do Books.

I knew if she called on me, I would mess up. Each person had to read a passage. We went around the circle. I was not a good reader, and those stupid books didn't make any sense to me.

Mr. Brown explained that he wanted Jason and those in that group to come up to the carpet for reading.

"Open your book to page 34. Let's do popcorn reading. Who would like to begin?"

A child began to read. When he came to a stopping place, he called out the name of a friend. The friend would continue reading, and the same procedure would continue. Periodically, Mr. Brown would make comments or ask questions to the group about the reading.

* * * * *

Teachers have more knowledge and understanding about how students learn and best teaching practices. For this reason, teaching practices have changed. The goal is never to ridicule or humiliate a student. The goal is to help students gain confidence in themselves and their learning. No longer are reading groups conducted like those above. Mrs. Butler's Red Robins were typical reading groups of thirty years ago. Mr. Brown's approach is representative of approximately ten years ago. Today, the approach is different. Research has provided more effective strategies, and more tools are available to make teaching better. Teachers certainly know what doesn't work and have determined approaches that do work. Here are a few of those basic practices that are effective:

- actively engage students in learning
- make learning meaningful
- vary the approach
- provide mini-lessons
- use a multisensory learning
- use authentic learning
- provide frequent feedback

There are strategies and practices that are designed for specific subject areas. For example, in reading, teachers now:

- utilize informal assessment—determine background knowledge
- ask questions—focus on meaning
- analyze the text structure
- visualize
- summarize
- listen to the reader
- encourage daily reading
- set the stage for success
- teach phonics but not totally
- provide multiple genres
- model reading and explain what you are thinking

- give choice
- provide a variety of levels
- teach reading strategies (name them)
- give value to reading
- support readers
- give readers opportunities to talk about their reading
- no worksheet or workbook.
- match reading to writing
- integrate curriculum (social studies, science, math, reading, writing)

Math teachers use manipulatives and make sure students have the perquisite skills required before going on to more complex areas. Here are some of the primary focus points for math:

- informally assessment—determine level of understanding prerequisite concepts
- give math value as it related to everyday life
- make it hands-on
- use manipulatives and visuals
- talk about the process
- use real life situations
- offer choice
- demonstrate the multiple ways to achieve the answer

Teaching policies have changed

Brandon strolled into the science class as if he knew it would be another interesting class filled with intentional actions aimed at tormenting the science teacher, Mr. Partner. Brandon was a typical student worried more about having fun than learning.

Mr. Partner sat at his desk as all the students entered the room. When everyone was seated, Mr. Partner began to pass out the classwork and provide explanations of the procedures for completing the assignment. As he wrote on the board to provide an illustration, he flinched as if suddenly stung by a bee. He touched his arm to see what would cause the pain. The class was very quiet.

Mr. Partner continued only to turn at the moment when a flying spitball hurdled down upon his head. His face red with anger, Mr. Partner looked about the room for the one who was so bold. There were no guilty expressions. Nevertheless, he had suspicions and would catch the one responsible.

Turning his back to the class once more, Mr. Partner quickly looked back at the class in time to see another spitball aimed at his shoulder. The shooter was revealed with the weapon still in hand.

"That's enough. I'll see you after class, Brandon, for three licks with the paddle."

Would this situation happen today? (It happened about fifty years ago.) Perhaps, but the student is very unlikely to receive three licks with a paddle. Unfortunately, today, we must worry about shootings with a real gun causing fatalities.

What has changed? Perhaps, the students have changed a little. The types of offenses are more sophisticated (technology issues, drugs, weapons), and the discipline is very different.

In today's classrooms, there are students who break rules or do not follow the norms, but the consequences do not include corporal punishment. Yesterday, students might be kept in at recess. Today, students are not allowed to miss recess (in many schools) because it takes away play time and a time to rest from academics. Today, a student may be playing a video game on his/her phone after repeatedly being told to stop. A teacher may remove the phone (temporarily) until the lesson is over. Many parents do not want their students without phones for the very practical reason of maintaining communication.

Brandon did something wrong, but the punishment may not have been appropriate for the crime. Trying to help students have a vested interest in the learning through ownership coupled with programs that teach respect for each other is the approach used in classrooms today.

Resource officers are on duty to make sure no laws are broken and order is maintained.

Students have changed

Nguyen sheepishly entered the classroom with his head lowered as he tried to speak. "Mi nam is Nguyen." Mrs. Ricks placed her hand on his shoulder and led him to a seat. "We are so happy to have you in our class, Nguyen," she said with a smile. "Can you tell us about yourself?"

Nguyen just stared as if he didn't understand the question. He said nothing. His sweet expression spoke kindness, but his body language demonstrated fear and uncertainty.

Nguyen is from Vietnam. He attends a school that is located near an army base. Many of the children in the school have parents who are in service. This year, there are five children (in the entire elementary school) who do not speak English. They will be helped by the resource teacher and the English-as-a-second-language teacher.

Would this happen today? (It happened about thirty-five years ago.) Yes, it would. However, one does not need to go to a military base to find children who do not speak English. Today, there are many, many children in schools across the country who do not speak the language. There are many more techniques used to assist the children; teachers are still overwhelmed by the numbers.

What about Nguyen's cultural difference? Did the teacher thirty-five years ago try to understand the cultural differences? Perhaps not. Teachers now realize that language differences certainly indicate cultural differences. Many classrooms today are filled with a very diverse population. The influx of immigrants necessitates the need for teachers to strive to bridge the gap in understanding between cultures and languages. However, sometimes, there are too many.

* * * * *

Jake walked into the kindergarten class. He was cute and neatly dressed. Looking around the room, he found his chair and sat down. Mrs. Toms began the morning duties while the children began their morning routine.

Without warning, the teacher was startled by the loud shouts from the front of the room. There was Jake with John in a "tug of war" over a purple pencil.

"It's mine," Jake screamed.

"It's mine," John began to explain. "My brother gave it to me."

Jake immediately ripped the pencil out of John's hand and hit him.

Mrs. Toms walked over to the boys and calmly whispered, "We can settle this without shouts or hitting."

"But it's mine!" Jake protested. I want my _____ pencil! If you don't make him give it to me, I'll beat his _____ and tell my daddy. He'll come here and beat your ____, too.

This happened within the last five years. Perhaps, the question is would this have happened twenty years ago? I don't think so. I taught special needs children and did not see this in any child so young. Young children were usually more intimidated by authority figures and less likely to be as bold as to confront a teacher or principal. However, our society has changed. Serious behavior problems with very young children are not uncommon now.

When Jake's mom was called in to talk about the situation, she explained that Jake never uses bad language, and the teacher must be mistaken. Moreover, Jake would never hit another child. She felt there was no reason to come in to talk because, obviously, Jake had done nothing wrong.

Today, some parents are not willing to consider that the child might be at fault or wrong. In the past, the child was wrong until proven different, not because the child was bad but because the child was a child. Today, parents are not as quick to consider the child might be wrong. Parents will listen to the explanation of a kindergarten child as compared to what was seen and heard by several adults.

Now, behavior problems are more serious and begin at an earlier age than in past years. Where the biggest threats in the past were fist fights, vandalism, or disrespect for authority, today, violence is a real threat ranging from cyberbullying and bullying to gangs and guns. We have a changing society.

Perhaps, the most upsetting change and new concern is with suicide among young students.

My son called today to tell me his concern about his daughter, Kayleigh. Kayleigh is thirteen, and she just found out her friend from kindergarten through fifth grade committed suicide. As upsetting as it is, this is the third child Kayleigh has known who committed suicide. Her closeness to the children varies, but these children go to her school. It's very much a reality for her.

As a grandmother, I am devasted for my granddaughter and extremely concerned about her feelings for her friends and the choice they made. As a teacher, I am surprised and worried about what is happening to our students in our changing society.

According to the Centers for Disease Control and Prevention (CDC), the suicide rate among young people (ten to twenty-four) has significantly increased by 56 percent. This alarming statistic is more evidence of a changing society. Suicide is the second most common death for children between the ages of ten to twenty-four.

What are the implications for teachers? I think this puts more pressure on teachers who care about their students to be more in tune to their behaviors and actions. Teachers want to notice any hint of a problem. Here are some warning signs:

- significant change in behavior
- depression
- conversations or actions of self-destruction
- taking extreme chances

These signs indicate intervention is needed. Contact the school counselor to confirm concerns. Then, she should notify the parents.

The Center for Suicide Prevention lists risk factors that are worth noting to ensure that students are not considering suicide:

- previous suicide attempt
- untreated depression (excessive aggression)
- untreated mental illness
- risk-taking behavior
- self-harm
- physical ailments
- drug abuse (or alcohol)
- exposure to violence or abuse (physical, emotional, sexual)
- family history of mental illness
- unstable family situation
- negative school experience (bullying)
- incomplete comprehension of death (finality)

What can a teacher do?

Teachers are only with their students part of the day. Often, what is seen at school is not what may be within the heart of a student. While teachers are limited in their time with students and as to what can be done, there are steps that can be taken to help. These suggestions go across the board in helping all students and are part of the essentials for teaching. Still, they are worth repeating:

- help students develop a positive self-esteem
- build solid and positive relationship with the student and with parents as much as possible
- help the students develop good problem-solving and coping skills
- encourage extracurricular activities at school
- pray

Conclusion

Our society is always changing. Some of those changes are powerful and are a wonderful means in helping teachers teach. In other cases, there is a price to pay for the improvements. For example, technology brings knowledge, entertainment, efficient communication, and makes our world smaller. The price we pay is a high one:

- Students are less active (video games).
- Students appear to have a shorter attention span.
- Pornography is readily accessible.
- A new type of aggressive behavior is introduced with cyberbullying.
- Chat rooms provide enticing means to seduce children and adults.
- Identity theft has become an easier crime.
- Everyone can know someone's business in a matter of minutes through social media.

In order to attempt to meet the needs of our changing students, we must be flexible, attentive, and lifelong learners, always seeking a better way to reach our students. We must look at society and the students within our classrooms to make sure we know what we need to do to teach them. Practices, policies, teacher roles, and students have drastically changed. As educators, we must be alert to what we see in order to guide students to new learning and a safe path to living. More importantly, *you will need to pray.*

Prayer

>Lord,
>
>Our world is changing so quickly. We, as adults,
>   struggle to keep up.
>Help me help the children be prepared for today
>   and tomorrow.
>Give me eyes to see their future needs and means
>   to help them in meeting those needs.
>Grant them abilities to succeed.
>Thanks be to God.
>Amen.

Something to make you smile

Many things change, but the blatant honesty of young children does not. One can't help but appreciate such.

"Mrs. Hawkins, did you get your hair cut?" Solomon asked while staring at my hair.

"Yes, I did," I confessed, anticipating a vote of approval from my young friend.

"Well, you shouldn't have," Solomon said with confidence.

8

Teacher, School, Parents, and Community: A Collaboration of Support

Larry was a shy, sweet little boy who was "easy to love." When he entered my classroom, I immediately recognized his neediness. His small, thin frame revealed a meager diet and hand-me-downs that hung on his body like they were from an older brother who was much larger. Despite his gaps in learning, Larry tried very hard to complete his work and do a good job. He wanted to please and sought his teacher's approval. Amazingly, Larry smiled a lot.

One day, we were doing a self-concept activity geared to build self-esteem. Using a large piece of paper, I asked students to allow me to trace their body on the paper. Afterward, they could pick out pictures from magazines of things they liked and paste them on to the life-sized picture of themselves. Most of the children enjoyed the activity. Larry was no exception as he eagerly positioned himself on the paper, and I began to draw around his frail body. Bringing the marker along his arm, I noticed places between the shoulder and elbow where the bone extended outward in an unnatural way. Also, between the elbow and hand, the bone curved. The same thing occurred on the legs. My thoughts raced as I tried to figure out why his outline was not "normal."

Larry was in a readiness class. After school, I went to talk with his teacher. I explained what happened. The teacher lowered her head and began.

"Larry comes in daily with injuries. Once, he came in with abrasions to his head. Apparently, his daddy hit him with a baseball bat. The injury was serious. I took him to the doctor where he was treated," the teacher explained *"Why hasn't DSS [Department of Social Services] been notified?"* I asked the teacher. *She explained that she had followed protocol and talked with the school nurse who is supposed to contract DSS. Unfortunately, the school nurse did not believe in contacting DSS.*

"I told the school nurse, but she said that life was different for them. When I persisted, finally a call was made, but by then, the family had moved," with sadness in her voice, the teacher said.

Based on what I heard from the teacher, I deducted Larry's bones were broken, and when left untreated, healed without being set, resulting in extensions in places where normally the bone would be straight. My heart sank.

This story happened many years ago. Today, teachers (and the school nurse) are required by law to notify the Department of Social Services (DSS) in such cases. The point of the story is to help teachers appreciate the urgency of having resources available to help them particularly in situations like that of Larry. Lacking true support, this outstanding (somewhat fearless) teacher took it upon herself to take the child to a doctor. She was committed to her students. She made a significant difference in the lives of many children. There are resources available today to help teachers in such terrible situations.

Bad things are still happening. Fears of litigation prohibit some people from getting involved. Fears of the problem being too large keep others from trying to help. But help is available where there is a strong alliance among teachers, school, parents, and community. Such an alliance allows for a break in the link (parent or school or community) and still have enough strength to attack the problem. With strong school personnel and a caring community with doctors who are willing to help without pay and fear of retribution, the problem can be attacked. Within the community are lawyers who are willing to help in "delicate" situations and expect no pay. Where do we begin?

We begin with the teacher. The teacher is the link between the student and the parents, between the parents and the school, and between the school and the community. "United we stand [and conquer], divided we fall [or fail]." Problems such as poverty, influx of children from other countries, child neglect, or child abuse do not have easy solutions. However, the chances of solving or making the situation better is increased when there is a joint effort or partnership. The teacher is a catalyst that can initiate change and bring about partnerships. In doing so, he/she must be the liaison between the school (or district) and parents and between the school (or district) and the community. Before a partnership can be established, there must be a clear indication of how the investment of time, resources, and energies are valuable to all participants.

- Determine what the school has in place to promote partnerships with parents and the community.
- Talk with administrators about appointing a committee of parents, business leaders/representatives, and teachers with goals of building relationships to establish a partnership.
- Within a designated room (established for parents/volunteers, see section on parents), set up an information center about the school and local businesses. Have cards, brochures, flyers from those businesses explaining their individual contribution to the partnership. Allow the community to be "part of the school." Decorate it with student's drawings and outstanding work. Have flyers that support those businesses that support the effort/school and post them in the room and throughout the community.
- Plan a day to invite the stakeholders in to see what is happening in the schools.

  1. Have students perform with music, art, poems, etc.
  2. Invite the members for breakfast or lunch (funding from PTO or sponsors?).

- Have displays throughout the school publicizing the joint ventures between the school and businesses.

- Find schools (elementary, middle, or high schools) within the state who have more resources and ask for them to become partners.
- Get students involved, help them see the value and benefits of everyone participating in the learning. Let them use art, music, and crafts to contribute to the publicity as the goal becomes to unite the community in a shared vision of productivity and achievement.

Poor schools within poor communities

Most schools are funded from the federal, state, and local money. Federal funding is just 10 percent and often targets low-income schools or special groups. State funding is based on a formula, and local funds are based on property taxes. Unfortunately, the poorer districts do not have the businesses to support the required tax, so the burden is upon the people who do not have enough money. It is even possible for a rich district to have a rural school with fewer business and a low-income base to have much less than another school located in town within the same district.

Efforts are being made to adjust the problem. However, because there are many low-income schools that lack materials, proper buildings, and the best teachers (poor working conditions discourage many), there is a different quality of education, and teaching in these circumstances is much more challenging. In these cases, it is even more critical that teachers work collaboratively with others to get help. The community must get involved.

A community is a group of people who live in the same area, have a shared vision, and vested interest in that area. Most of us want the same type of community—one that is safe, healthy, with caring people who have the same goals for the area, with convenient establishments (churches and businesses), and clean surroundings. Unfortunately, such an environment is fueled and maintained by money and a partnership or alliance made up of those who want to establish and maintain such an area. Having an income (money) is the primary driving force for making healthy, productive communities. The second controlling force is people who care and are willing to invest time and energy into such an endeavor. Lacking these funds or the people who share this vision will leave a previously flourishing community desolate and infested with crime, dilapidated buildings, and vacant lots.

All the members of a community are stakeholders with a vested interest in having a healthy community. Those communities that lack businesses, resources, and people who care about the area are often communities struck with poverty. Because each member of the community is profoundly impacted by the poison of poverty, actions to combat the situation must be determined and implemented. The first step is the identification of the problem.

- When identifying the problem of poverty in the community, one needs to remember that communities vary, and the level and extent of the problem can vary as well. Each community need to assess the needs of the given area and identify the problem in terms of needs. For example, the high crime rate in the area warrants a need for more police patrolling the area.
- The massive influx of immigrants in the schools and communities has made it difficult for teachers to meet the needs of so many students from various backgrounds (Ferris and Raley 2016).
- Overcrowded classes and difficulties with classroom management make finding good teachers difficult. (Obidah and Howard 2005).
- The poverty rate is at 15 percent in our country (Communities, Individuals, and the Long Fight Against Poverty 2014).
- Communities with people who lack resources can quickly become high-crime areas. Those who have resources move out of the area, leaving a devastating community with a depleted economy (Environmental Systems Research Institute 2016).

- Those businesses still in the area begin to fail or relocate because profits are low, and crime is high (Environmental Systems Research Institute 2016).
- Because of the danger with the increased level of crime, lack of funding for the schools, and difficulty in securing qualified teachers, the educational opportunities are not equal to those in neighborhoods with more resources.
- Statistics indicate more youth in the poverty areas do not graduate from high school.

The suggested actions listed below involve various members of the stakeholders. In some cases, the actions are better accomplished by teachers, students, administrators, parents, community members, or a joint committee made up of some of the previously mentioned people.

- Present the problem in a meeting with businesses and community members to plan and implement strategies that would involve parents and businesses with specific goals to benefit all stakeholders in the partnership. Extend and enhance any program that is in place giving value to any investments made by businesses.
- Give the community voice and communicate the value of the program to the community through words that make the community inclusive. For example, we want our community to grow and provide economic flourishment for all. Here is the concern: our businesses are not showing profit, our students are not motivated to learn because they do not see the value in learning, our streets are dangerous, and we do not seem to find those who can help, so we must try to make things better together.
- Provide specific levels of involvement for each group within the community to be actively involved in the solution. Clean up the community. Fix up the community. Make up your minds to make it better.

- Focus on business leaders and establish regular meetings to share insights and brainstorm specific solutions to key concerns. Give them a voice in the process of educating students in preparation for them becoming contributing members of society and future employees of these establishments. While the leaders are the focus, the invitation should be extended to parents, educators, business leaders, and any stakeholder in the community. Develop committees where various stakeholders are involved not only in the basic level, but also in the leadership roles.

- Make the partnership beneficial for all participants. Let the students (who want to do so) help clean up the area around a business. "Build a Better Business" day means students helping community members with whatever project is feasible and safe. Times and the supervision of children can be coordinated through the Parent Teacher Associate at school.

- Build a foundation/structure to sustain and maintain the support system through ongoing communication Make those in the community aware of what is happening in the schools and businesses.

- Let students use their art skills to make advertisement signs for those businesses that are supportive of the school. Proudly display those signs in the establishments.

- Provide education. Offer courses in parenting and specific educational programs that can benefit those in the community, self-concept development, managing a budget, gardening, etc. Solicit members of the community to share their talents as leaders of these activities.

- Look for grants, charities, and other sources of income to support the effort.

- Contact the local college or university, asking that they form a partnership with the school. Professional development school partnerships can be established without fees from the school. Such a partnership can be an asset to all participants.

- Provide free advertisement within the school via posters, newsletters etc., for businesses contributing to various projects (flower garden, science projects materials, etc.).
- Have special days where the community/businesses are recognized and honored for their help. Focus on student lead activities—lunch, music, speeches, arts, etc.
- Include the businesses that help with free publicity in school newspapers, websites, and word of mouth.
- Pass out flyers to doctor's offices, various medical centers, etc. educational opportunities within the school to learn about what is happening and/or to volunteer within the school.
- Establish specific goals that have clearly identified roles of all within the partnerships.
- Establish places where information about the school can be posted on a regular basis. The information may include parenting classes, screening for high-risk students, needs, concerns, celebrations, and any other information that may prove pertinent or beneficial to stakeholders.
- Submit a short survey to parents and businesses to determine how better to unite the community.
- Include community members and businesses in PTA meetings.

Joyce Epstein (2004) explains the need for a school learning community, "A school learning community includes educators, students, parents, and community partners who work together to improve the school and enhance students' learning opportunities," and a hierarchy of various levels of involvement. The greater the involvement, the more binding the partnership. She explains six levels of involvement:

- *Parenting. Assist families with parenting skills, family support, understanding child and adolescent development, and setting home conditions to support learning at each age and grade level. Assist schools in understanding families' backgrounds, cultures, and goals for children.*

- *Communicating. Communicate with families about school programs and student progress. Create two-way communication channels between school and home.*

- *Volunteering. Improve recruitment, training, activities, and schedules to involve families as volunteers and as audiences at the school or in other locations. Enable educators to work with volunteers who support students and the school.*

- *Learning at home. Involve families with their children in academic learning at home, including homework, goal setting, and other curriculum-related activities. Encourage teachers to design homework that enables students to share and discuss interesting tasks.*

- *Decision-making. Include families as participants in school decisions, governance, and advocacy activities through school councils or improvement teams, committees, and parent organizations.*

- *Collaborating with the community. Coordinate resources and services for families, students, and the school with community groups, including businesses, agencies, cultural and civic organizations, and colleges or universities. Enable all to contribute service to the community"* (Educational Leadership, May 2004, volume 61, number 8).

- *Schools as Learning Communities* (pages 12–18).

Conclusion

Perhaps, it does "take a village to raise a child." Certainly, it may in those cases where parents do not have all the resources necessary to meet the needs of the child. In those cases, a collaboration is required among all those who can make a difference in the child's life, beginning with the teacher (to initiate the collaboration), the parents, the school, and the community. Helping the community see the value in a unified partnership is the first step in working together. The need to establish a strong community partnership with the school is an essential factor in attacking the problem in a joint manner. There are specific actions that must be taken by the teacher, school, and community. The more involved the parents are, the better the chance for total involvement by the community.

First, parents must be made aware of the option to work together. They need to join in identifying solutions to the problem. Next, ongoing communication and collaboration must be established. Groups of community members, parents, and school members must see value in their efforts and a reward at the end of the journey. Finally, a system must be put in place that will sustain the partnership allowing for voice for each stakeholder to be part of the ongoing communication with a shared vision for a better tomorrow today. You need to pray!

Prayer

Lord,

Help us unite together to help children.
Let us find resources that have the means
To make a difference in poor schools and communities.
Let us have a shared vision and help us achieve that goal.
Thank You, Father.
Amen.

A reason to smile

Both our sons were active boys climbing trees, playing ball, and riding bicycles. It was not uncommon for them to get skinned up playing, despite my warnings to be more careful. Our youngest son, Ashton, was about ten when within a year's time, he broke his arm two times. He broke it once from jumping over a bush in the front yard and another time while riding his bicycle.

Once again, his arm was hurt, and he needed to be taken to have his arm checked. I took him to the emergency room. After the doctor looked over his file, he began to look at me in a questioning and somewhat accusing manner. After looking back over the records, the doctor quickly looked straight at Ashton and began, "Hello, Ashton. How are you today?"

Ashton nonchalantly replied, "I guess I'm okay, but my arm hurts."

Continuing at times to glare at me, the doctor turned to Ashton, looking intently as if to make sure he did not miss a response and asked, "How did you hurt your arm?"

Ashton spoke without a pause, "It's my mom's fault!"

My heart sank. Here I am, a loving mother and would never dream of causing such horrible harm on our son. I looked at Ashton and was speechless.

The doctor, not surprised, looked over at me as if he had found the culprit and continued, "Ashton, what did you mom do?"

Ashton did not hesitate with his answer, "She made me clean out my closet, and I fell off the stool when I was trying to reach the top."

9

Crisis in the Schools

The public address system began to make the scratchy noises, indicat-ing an announcement was at hand. Mr. Tanner, the principal, began, "At this time, we will have a tornado drill." Shortly after he made the announcement, the phone rang, and we were told that there is a tornado warning for this area. The "drill" is not really a drill.

My mind frantically searched my brain to figure out if I needed to take these children inside. My classroom was located next to the main building. The metal building seemed to creak and strain as I heard the wind push against the side of the faded, heavily used trailer. While the district had more resources than many other districts in our state, the population in this area was growing too fast to accommodate the needs or the vast numbers of students. As a result, many teachers throughout the district were housed in trailers. Some of the trailers were older. Mine was one of those older trailers.

Strong winds pushed against the side of the building, and the chil-dren began to look at me through the eyes of fear. As a resource teacher, I had been told since my room was outside, it was my call to decide when we needed to come inside as a result of bad weather. These were young children ranging from ages five to seven. They were such sweet children, always polite and cooperative, easy to love. I could see the trust in their eyes. They would do whatever Mrs. Hawkins said.

"We are just fine, boys and girls. Let's play a game," I said enthu-siastically. "Take the hand of a neighbor and hold on tight. Let's see who

can hold on tight as we go into the building. Don't let go. Winners are those who hold on tight and make it all the way inside the building." My voice was strong and confident, just like a teacher's voice should be.

I headed toward the door with my little line of students, all holding on with smiles, eagerly waiting to play the game. "God, please be with us and protect these children. Help us make it inside safely," I prayed with all my heart.

The wind fought me as I tried to open the door. Finally, I held it open enough to get us through and begin the walk to the main building. It wasn't too far, about fifty feet. But these were young children with not a lot of strength. Immediately, I wondered if I had made a good choice— staying in the old trailer with questionable structural reliability, or fighting the winds holding on to the children in a hand chain that may break, releasing the small children to be at the mercy of the wind like ragdolls.

I held my breath as we slowly and methodically began the trek. I could see the chain begin to wave as some of the children fell back. While holding on to the hand of the child near me, I stepped back to support the child at the end of the line.

Finally, I was pulling the door of the heavy building and eagerly pushing the children inside. We made it safe and sound, *I thought to myself. Mattie exclaimed, "We all won! We didn't break the chain." All I could think was,* Thank God. *In my best teacher voice, I rejoiced with Mattie and said, "Yes, we are all winners."*

*****

"I wonder what time the lockdown will begin?" Mrs. Rainy questioned with an expression that shared her dread.

"I don't know, but I know that my entire class cannot fit in that bathroom again." Mrs. Frank sighed. "You can't fit twenty-three kids in a bathroom and still breath," she continued. "Besides, it's not healthy, and it really stinks in there. As soon as we get settled, one kid will need to use the bathroom. We can't just let a child use the toilet in front of all the other children. Who wants to ask a six-year-old to hold it? I mean, really, do you feel lucky?"

"Well, don't forget the lockout right after," Mrs. Boozer reminded.

"That's easier. We just all get out of sight and lock our doors. We still have those students who, all of a sudden, have to go to the bathroom at that exact moment, but at least we can go on with our work," Mrs. Rainy explained.

*****

"Yeah, no school for the next two whole weeks!" Martha squealed. "I can't wait!"

The president had made the announcement, explaining the take-over in Asia of the virus and asking everyone to stay at home. The highly contagious coronavirus had started to spread into our country. It was just a matter of time. Then the governor closed the schools.

Martha's mother could not hide her anxieties as her mind was bombarded with questions and concerns. What would they do if they can't go to work, go to the mall, or get out? What is going to happen? Everyone is potentially contagious! This virus is real and is killing people. What about my parents? What about Martha? Who is supposed to teach her? I certainly can't do that!

Children see the news and know the fear in their parents. They are affected by this crisis.

These stories depict three different types of crises that can drastically affect the school. What is a crisis? A crisis is any unpredictable event that poses danger, intense trouble, or difficulty. Such situations can threaten the safety of students and significantly modify their routines. Teachers know that students do not like any change in routines. Routines provide security and assurance of what to expect.

Whether it is a school intruder, a pandemic, or life-threatening weather conditions, it is up to the teacher to protect and help the students remain calm in the midst of such "storms." When the decision is made for the school to close, the responsibility goes back to the parents until the children return to school. Our society is changing; we have more of these types of emergencies, and we must be prepared mentally, emotionally, spiritually, and physically to deal with them. What can a teacher do?

Weather Crises

According to the World Resource Institute (2019), the extreme weather has become more frequent and severe over the last decade. These severe weather conditions have caused more than four hundred billion dollars in damages.

These are the top ten most server weather conditions in the US over the last ten years:

- Hurricane Harvey (2017)—Record-breaking rainfall killing sixty-eight people.
- Hurricane Sandy (2012)—"Frankenstorm" called because it was so intense and one of the most damaging storms to the East Coast of all time.
- Hurricane Maria (2017)—Landfall in Southeast Puerto Rico after major destruction to Saint Croix, causing ninety billion dollars in damages and responsible for nearly three thousand deaths.
- Hurricane Irma (2017)—Category 5 storm (later downgraded to category 4), causing roughly fifty billion dollars in damages to US Virgin Islands and Florida Keys.
- Heat and drought (2012)—Heat and drought killing crops and reducing lake (and river) water levels, costing about thirty-four billion dollars in agricultural losses.
- Tornado (2011)—Outbreak of over 200 tornadoes across the Southeast, killing 321 people (most in Alabama).
- Drought in the Southern Plains (2010–2011)—Affecting Texas, Oklahoma, New Mexico, Arizona, Kansas, and Louisiana, the drought resulted in ninety-five heat-related deaths.
- California winds, heat, and wildfires (2017–2019)— The strongest and most devasting was the Camp Fire in Northern California in 2018.
- Hurricane Michael (2018)—Category 5 hurricane killed fifty-seven people and cost roughly twenty-five billion dollars when it made landfall near Panama City, Florida.

- California drought (2012–2015)—This drought was the worst in nearly forty years, bringing wildfires, water shortages, and agricultural losses.

There were extreme weather conditions prior to this time, but these are significantly more critical. Earlier, they were not as frequent or as severe. Unfortunately, experts agree that it appears these catastrophes are increasing in severity and frequency every year. Fortunately, the death tolls are down because of improved forecasting and communicating. This doesn't change the predicted increase.

I share this information, not to make teachers fearful, but rather to help them be aware and prepared. While students attend school 170 to 180 days (depending on the state) each year or between 47 and 49 percent of the calendar year, the chances are very good they will be at school when such a crisis may occur. Every teacher is very familiar with the protocol for each extreme weather situation. Because of regular practice, the students are more than familiar with the procedures. The administrators do only so much and are guided by the district office with respect to regulations and course of action. However, it's the teacher who is at the main front. The teacher controls the students, sets the emotional level, and guides the students to safety. So what does this mean for the teacher that there are sure to be more days with extreme weather conditions? It means the teacher needs to pray, maintain control, and be calm.

School Intruders / Shootings

It is hard to believe school shootings have been going on for centuries. The earliest recorded school shooting occurred in 1764, where Lenape American Indians entered the schoolhouse, shot and killed the schoolmaster and nine to ten children (reports vary). Then, in the 1800s, there were eleven recorded shootings. From those, eight people were killed. The first three decades of the twentieth century had very few reports of mass or multiple shootings. The three most violent attacks on schools involved either arson or explosions. Then, beginning the 1930s, there were approximately six shootings with eleven deaths. In the forties, there were about ten shootings with thirteen deaths. Following in the fifties, there were fifteen shootings and twelve deaths. In the sixties, there were eleven shootings with thirty-four deaths (one mass murder). In the seventies, there were three mass shootings. There were a total of five shootings, with seventeen deaths in the seventies. In the eighties, there was a major increase in school shootings to include a hostage situation, where 150 students were held hostage. One of the perpetrators accidentally set off a bomb, killing herself and injuring seventy-eight students. Over a four-year period (1986–1990), 71 people were killed and 201 injured. Overall, in the eighties, about ten shootings occurred, with approximately ninety killed.

By the nineties, school shootings were not as unusual. There were over 240 deaths resulting from school shootings. From 2000 through 2010, there were 147 deaths from school shootings in the United States.

Obviously, these crises are more frequent and devastating. With modern technology and understanding, one can't help but ask: Have things improved since then? We have resource officers and metal detectors in the schools. It is sad to report that in the last ten years, we have had over four hundred (427) deaths from school shootings in the United States. What does this mean for the future? It means that no matter how much we try to install metal detectors, have resource officers on site, and inspect students' belongings, it is still possible that a threat can occur at a school. With this in mind, the teacher is still the significant one. The teacher is the one on the front lines, who tries to be between the student and the line of danger. Since I have never been in such a terrifying predicament, I cannot speak with authority, nor can I assure you that I can implement what I know to be sound judgment. However, I know that with God's help, I can do what I need to do to ensure the safety and well-being of everyone.

Pandemic—Coronavirus (COVID-19)

Diseases have been around as long as the human race existed. However, a disease that takes over a country, then a continent, and finally the globe has not occurred very often and certainly not recently. Cholera, bubonic plague, smallpox, and influenza are some of the most brutal killers in human history. The most recent outbreak of the Ebola virus (killed thousands of people) was confined to West Africa. In 2005 to 2012, the HIV/AIDS virus killed thirty-six million people. Going back a while, in 1968, the "Hong Kong Flu" killed one million people throughout the Philippines, India, Australia, Europe, and the United States.

As of the writing of this book, our country and the entire world are devastated by the coronavirus (COVID-19). Most of us living today have never encountered such a disease paralyzing our country and dramatically altering our daily routine. The coronavirus has pushed educators into a corner and demanded a system be in place to meet the needs of all the students since they cannot attend the school. Teachers are scrambling to put together lesson plans that are meaningful yet need little or no direct instruction. Parents are embracing the challenges of teaching their children and, at the same time, looking at the role of the teacher in a very new light. The parents are realizing that teaching is not quite as easy as they think.

While parents are doing their best they can, the fact of the matter is most of the children will not make the progress that is expected. Next year, teachers will be able to see how well the parents have fared as educators. Fortunately, there are no evaluations. However, as the students advance to the next grade or level, they will arrive less prepared than planned. Perhaps those who will suffer the most are the younger children who need more structured, hands-on activities, and concrete items (math manipulatives) to conceptualize and internalize the learning. Parents are not prepared to provide such instruction. These kindergarteners and first graders need activities that break tasks into components, making them more understandable. Some of the little ones may need a lot of "review" next year before new and more complex skills can be learned. That problem will be dealt with next year, when the teachers quickly realize the gaps in learning.

New crises bring new problems. While not every teacher is as creative as the next, teachers are great problem solvers. That's what they do every single day. The problems vary in size and difficulty, but they are present. As the challenges develop, teachers can and will be successful. Dedicated teachers will persevere and "learn as they go" as they become proficient in this endeavor. Because that is what teachers do!

The world is changing. Extreme weather is more prevalent. School crises occur more frequently. Presently, a pandemic is raging through our country, and other unforeseen crises may occur. What does this mean for teachers? It means teachers must be ready for anything and embrace the reality that we live in a changing world. Specifically, what can teachers do? Many items listed below are common sense. Through the years, I have found common sense is not common. Understandings are built upon experiences, and everyone does not encounter the same situations, nor do they handle those situations the same way. Hopefully, the suggestions listed below will serve to help or bring to mind other thoughts on dealing with crises.

- *Pray.* Catastrophes will continue to occur as they have since the beginning of time. Unfortunately, we are seeing more than in the past. Pray for God's protection for you and your students. Ask God to provide guidance that you might do the right thing in all situations.

- *Remain calm regardless of the crisis.* Students are very perceptive, and they know their teachers well. They will respond with the same level of anxiety and fear as the teacher. Often, they can read any emotion that the teacher has. For this reason, it is very important that the calm, relaxed disposition of the teacher be genuine, even if way down deep, there is great fear.

- *Be prepared for unexpected behaviors by both adults and students.* Disasters, emergencies, and various crises seem to bring out the worst in some people and the best in others. People may respond in anyway, at any time, that may be contrary to their typical behavior. A teacher must be prepared for such extreme actions.

- *Follow the designated procedures.* All schools have procedures in place for such situations. If something occurs (and it may), that is outside those planned procedures; teachers need to use their experience, common sense, and help from God to do what is best.

- *Be sensitive to those who are obviously upset and fearful.* Some students may need more reassurance and comfort than others. Be accommodating in these situations.
- *Have a plan for all possible scenarios that do not follow the norm.* For example, what will you do with a sick student or an adult who loses control?
- *Demonstrate your belief that all is well and all will be well through your body language, smiles, and words.*
- *If you are waiting for the "storm" to clear, or for instructions or guidelines on what to do next, keep students occupied as much as possible with stories, riddles, reviews, or educational games requiring little movement.* The less time for students to think about the situation, the better. Make it as "normal" as possible. In school, you do school things.
- *Transitions are the most difficult.* If moving from one room to another, or one place to another have a plan for the best possible movement. Ensure that all students will be accountable when reaching your destination. Having partners to help keep track of all students can be a good plan. For younger students, holding hands is a good approach.
- *Be mentally and emotionally prepared for anything.*
- *Be watchful, alert, and pray regularly.*

Because of the coronavirus, parents see teaching in a completely different "light." In one short week, many parents appear to have a deeper appreciation of teachers. Being both a teacher and parent of two boys, I found early on that teaching my own children was the hardest teaching I've ever experienced. My husband, blessed with many talents (patience of which is not one of those talents) would crash and burn within ten minutes of interacting with the boys. They would be in tears, and he would ask for hard whiskey. Consequently, I was eager to see what parents, who found themselves quarantined

and forced to teach elementary-age students, would find. This is
what I discovered:

- Many parents are like my husband and resort to alcohol to
  maintain sanity while teaching their children.
- Math is not a strong suit for most parents, particularly the
  use of lattice multiplication, partial sums, partial differences, partial products, partial quotients, or partial anything. Frustration is just the beginning to explaining what
  is felt by all involved.
- Some parents asked teachers if their children are difficult in
  class or if this unruly, uncooperative, almost disrespectful
  "I don't understand" behavior just something that they save
  and share with their parents at home. One parent explained
  that on the first day, the paddle had to come out just to
  keep siblings from disagreeing. After that, it got better.
- The refrigerator appears to be a distractor. Very frequently,
  students feel the need to inspect what foods are available in
  the refrigerator. Upon asking the child if he/she does this
  at school, the child responds, "No." To solve the problem,
  some parents suggest the students use their "school stomach" to avoid frequent trips to the kitchen.
- While multitasking might have been a skill of many parents prior to homeschooling, apparently, it was immediately lost during this experience. Teaching is all that feel
  humanly possible. Parents feel they have had a productive
  day if the children get out of bed, get dressed, and work on
  schoolwork for an hour. Nothing else is accomplished by
  the students or parents.
- Finally, it comes to my mind that perhaps the biggest problem is that parents are, in fact, not teachers. My cousin is a
  very successful businessman, greatly admired by many. He
  will not hesitate to tell me that he can teach and anyone
  can. "You just stand up there and tell a story." I love him
  dearly, so I just ignore his comment. As I know and every
  teacher knows, there is so very much more to teaching than

just saying, "Here's the information. Here's the book. Do the work." Now parents understand this too!

Conclusion

I've heard it said that there is nothing new under the sun (Solomon in Ecclesiastes). This means whatever the crisis may be, it has happened before; perhaps in a more complex way. People, through mankind, have dealt with crises. It may be new to our generation or society as a whole, but it has probably happened in the past. Learning from history is always a good practice to being, to understand, and to avoid the mistakes of others. I am confident that history will leave lessons for future generations. I hope they will embrace them as I hope and pray that we learn from the past, press on to the future, and face tomorrow with hope, love, and God.

Even though it may not seem feasible, the chances are good that more things may occur that are not typical. Everyone must plan for the worst and pray for the best. As a teacher being on the front lines of whatever occurs, it is paramount to realize the uncertainty in life, the unexpected and bizarre behavior in people and situations, and count on God to guide, protect, and bless us. We do live in a changing world. For this reason, the best plan is to pray.

Prayer

"Heavenly Father,

Bless the educators who walked into the classrooms, never knowing what might happen.
Give them insights to be able to do what is best in the event of unforeseen events.
Help them have the strength when needed, the wisdom as required, and the faith in those crises to know that you can handle whatever happens.
Amen.

Something to make you smile

One cannot help but laugh, as during this catastrophic pandemic, people are hording toilet papers. The symptoms of the virus have nothing to do with stomach problems. It is a respiratory infection. My husband explains it with a saying: "Common sense ain't a flower that blooms in every garden!"

During the coronavirus pandemic, my husband went to the grocery store to pick up a few groceries. He was walking down the paper isle to find some paper towels and saw blank shelves all around. Particularly obvious to him was the empty shelves of toilet paper. He smiled and wondered again why people are obsessed with toilet paper. Fortunately, he was not looking for toilet paper. As he continued to walk down the aisle, an elderly man walked closer to him and whispered softly under his breath, "Walmart just received a truckload of toilet paper. There's plenty there." My husband, who is seldom speechless, mumbled an appreciative "thank you" to the nice gentleman as he was obviously trying to help.

10

A Defining Moment

"Your profession is not what brings home your weekly paycheck, your profession is what you're put here on earth to do, with such passion and such intensity that it becomes spiritual in calling" (Vincent Van Gogh Kushandwizdom).

* * * * *

Tammy was only five and very excited about being in kindergarten. Today, her class would go to music for the first time. There was so much to see in the large room. There were musical instruments, bright posters, and little chairs. Tammy's eyes couldn't take it all in as she followed the other children slowly filing into the room.

Immediately, Mrs. Lowman welcomed the children. Mrs. Lowman was an excellent music teacher. Her love of music, children, and teaching resonated throughout the room and in all that she did. After she shared with the children all they would be doing in music, she noticed a little going up.

Finally, after surveying everything very carefully, Tammy looked at Mrs. Lowman and spoke with wonder, "Where is your bed?"

* * * * *

Both teachers and students sometimes think the school is the where teachers live. Dedication and determination find caring teach-

128

ers investing long hours and precious time away from family members to help students. Such commitment is admirable but must be done in moderation. Many great teachers have left the profession from "burn out" from trying so hard that they have depleted resources, energy, ideas, and desires. Because teaching is such a draining experience both physically and emotionally, teachers must have systems in place to replenish their energy and rejuvenate their commitment. They must take care of themselves and have a priority of God, family, self, and job. An improper order of these can result in a great loss in relationships or physical/emotional health. Support systems, proper diet, health, and hobbies are a good beginning for those who want to stay in the profession and be successful.

Teachers must face the reality that all problems will not be solved. Every child may not achieve the level of success that you think is best for the child. Do what you can to the best of your abilities. Be a lifelong learner, always striving for self-improvement and pray. When working with students, remember, when in doubt, do what you would do with your own child, always looking for what is best for the student.

In summary, focus your teaching on the following:

- Make students feel secure, respected, and appreciated. Let them know you care.
- Set up an environment that is cheerful, exciting, and encourages learning.
- Maintain strong communication between the teacher and the parents. Help parents develop a partnership with the teacher as advocates and support systems for their students.
- Let students share the responsibility of their learning. Set up academic goals that are reasonable providing success, but not making it too easy.
- Model (be cognizant of what you say and do) appropriate social interaction with students and other teachers. Eyes are always watching.
- Make learning fun. Incorporate food into the mix when possible. Be silly sometimes. It's okay to enjoy the learning.

- Choose your battles (with everyone in your life). Some things are not worth the strife it will cause.
- Set up situations for laughter (at appropriate times). Perhaps, the most effective tool to decrease stress and provide enjoyment in learning is laughter. Use funny read-alouds, look for humor in everyday situations, and share those funny moments from your family with the class. It makes you human and the experience fun.

Teachers are the action that fuels change to help themselves, the students, the parents, the school, and community as they teach all types of students and as advocates of these students and their parents. Teachers can make a difference. It begins with a positive attitude that is contagious. It continues with determination and commitment. It ends with pray.

* * * * *

"Mrs. Hawkins, there is someone here to see you," the secretary whispered over the loudspeaker. "I will send her to your room."

In a few minutes, an attractive young woman entered the room. I stared, not certain who she was, although she looked vaguely familiar.

"Mrs. Hawkins, don't you remember me?" the lady asked with an expression that begged for a yes answer.

"You look so familiar. Please tell me your name," I explained.

"My name is Terri Smith," she said with a smile.

"Oh, my goodness! It is so wonderful to see you again."

Immediately, my mind went back years to the shy little third grader. Her adorable face was framed with shoulder-length light-brown hair with bangs that almost seemed too short. Terri worked hard, was always polite, and tried her best responding well to all of my efforts to help her excel, despite her struggle with a learning disability.

"What are you doing now, Terri?" I asked.

"I'm a teacher, Mrs. Hawkins. I wanted to be a teacher, just like you," she sheepishly replied. I had to see you and just let you know how much I appreciate what you did for me.

I did make a difference in a child's life. My heart sang.

* * * * *

Terri's visit was a wonderful confirmation that I was doing what I was supposed to be doing. I knew that teaching was my calling, but I am like any other teacher where I had good days and not so good days. There were days when I felt I made no difference. There were days when I feared the difference that I had made, and there were fantastic days when I felt like I have made a significant difference in helping children. Not unlike parenting, teaching is a job where you don't really know if you've done a good job until it's too late to do anything about it. You just pray.

* * * * *

Several years ago, on the first day of school, Susie entered my fourth-grade classroom. She had long brown hair and brown eyes that searched the room carefully, as if looking for the perfect nook. Susie had several friends in my class. Her friends were more outgoing and confident. Susie was shy and somewhat reserved. Right from the beginning and throughout the year, she appeared to love being in my class despite the challenges she experienced academically. The expectations for the fourth-grade were higher than those put upon her in the past. Susie reluctantly complied, but she made sure her mother knew every difficult task that she endured. I invested much energy and strategies to make sure that Susie had every opportunity to grow and learn.

Of course, her mother made it a point to contact me regularly, expressing her concerns because Susie was stressed over the demands of being in the fourth-grade. Initially, her calls were polite, seeking understanding on my part about the "unrealistic" expectations put upon her "sweet little girl." Soon, the calls changed into stronger accusations that I was an uncaring teacher.

With much prayer and God's help, I maintained a professional stance, confident attitude, and supportive disposition toward the mother. I do not think I was Susie's mother's favorite person, but she tolerated me.

131

At the end of the year, Susie's test scores revealed marked progress. On the last day of school, Susie's mother approached me with arms out-stretched and a smile on her face. "Mrs. Hawkins, this has been Susie's best year. Thank you so much for being such a wonderful teacher!"

Not until the last day of school did Susie's mom realize that what I was trying to do was in Susie's best interest. Sometimes, other mom's like Susie's never see that what is happening is in the child's best interest. I would not have been able to survive the mother's con-stant calls, notes, surprise visits, and demands for special consider-ation for her child without God's help. The key is to allow God to work in your heart while trying very hard to maintain a professional stance at all times. Trust that God will prevail. He did.

* * * * *

When teaching special education, new children moved into the area regularly. Johnny was assigned to my class in the middle of the school year. We had not yet received records on him, so I just focused on establishing a great rapport and doing informal assessment. Johnny was a blond-haired, blue-eyed third grader who appeared energetic and eager to please. He and I got along well. He worked very hard and got along well with other children. Time passed, and we still hadn't gotten his records, so I just began to plan a program for him and continued working. Johnny had no apparent problems and seem to have adjusted to the new school, teachers, and classmates very well. He was helpful and polite. I felt fortunate to have him in my room. He started progressing academically and doing a great job in my classroom.

Finally, the records arrived. The files were very thick for a child who had only been receiving special services for two years. I began read-ing. It was unbelievable that these people were talking about the same child. According to the records, Johnny was emotionally handicapped with aggressive and defiant tendencies. His academic level was below his potential and grade level. Countless situations where Johnny had difficulties with children, teachers, and administrators were recorded. Johnny continued the year with great progress and behavior. He was a good student.

The point is twofold. First, do not solely base your assessment of a student on the opinions made by others. The way Johnny interacts with one does not dictate the way he will interact with all. Environments can significantly influence behavior. People can influence behaviors.

Second, remember God does miracles every day. Prayers for students make a big difference. It did for Johnny, and it did for me.

In closing, teachers have a tremendous job with overwhelming responsibility, but they have equally as tremendous an opportunity to profoundly affect the lives of many. It took years before I realized the power that a teacher has. Once teachers realize that power, they either use it very wisely or they use it destructively. If having been called to teach, the teacher knows he/she is accountable to a higher power (other than an administrator), that power being God. Knowing that, when coupled with prayer, the power can become a superpower.

According to dictionary.com (2020), a defining moment is "a point at which the essential nature or character of a person, group, etc. is revealed or identified." Perhaps, that is the defining moment for a teacher. The moment that a teacher realizes that teaching is his/her calling and that all things are possible through prayer. At that time, teaching becomes a superpower.

Prayer

Dear Father,

Thank You for the opportunity to teach.
Let me be every aware of my responsibilities to
    You and to these students
To be an advocate, helper, and encourager.
Help me to have wisdom, truth, and love
So that I might know what to do
And do it in love.
Thank You for giving me power beyond my
    understanding or abilities to teach.

Thank You for always helping me help others.
Amen.

Something to make you smile

Ashton, our youngest son had been helping me set up my classroom for a new school year. Each time I would count desks and set them up, I would be notified that another student had been moved to my class. Ashton who was only about 7 was growing tired of dragging desks into my room to accommodate the added students. Finally, I saw him getting pencil and paper and making the following sign that he proudly taped outside the door:

No Vacancy

APPENDIX A

EXIT SLIP
Name_____ Date_____
Today we talked about _____
Something new that I learned is
_____
_____
I need some help understanding _____
_____

Sample Exit Slip

Sample "goodie notes"

> *To the parents of*
> *I just wanted to take the time to let you know what a joy it is to work with _____.*
> *I help him with math. He is polite and tries hard. I appreciate his good manners. He is such a very sweet boy.*

> *To the parents of*
> *I just want to take a moment to let you know what a great job _____ has been doing in after school math class. Yesterday, she was on task, showed good manners, tried to do her best, and got most of her work correct. I so appreciate her hard work.*

APPENDIX B

American Girl Club

Have an inviting room

Supply plenty of books

Provide refreshments

Display the prize

Award the prize

APPENDIX C

Resources for helping those in poverty

Federal assistance programs are available for families who qualify for help. Some of these programs include:

- Supplemental Security Income Program (SSI) (disabilities)
- unemployment insurance
- Earned Income Tax Credit (EITC) (tax credit)
- Medicaid
- Children's Health Insurance Program (health care)
- Supplemental Nutrition Assistance Program (SNAP)
- The Special Supplemental Food Program for Women, Infants, and Children
- Child Nutrition Program (free or reduced lunch)
- Temporary Assistance for Needy Families (TANF)
- Affordable Care Act (health coverage through Medicaid)
- subsidized house, housing vouchers, and public housing programs
- Low-Income Home Energy Assistance Program (LIHEAP)
- Head Start (early childhood education)
- Federal Pell Grant Program (college and trade school grants)
- Lifeline program by Federal Communications Commission (FCC) (discounted landline and cell phone service)
- federal grants

- McKinney-Vento—National Center for Homeless Education (federally funded program that ensures homeless children have a right to go to school)

State and county agencies have funding, organizations, and services available for those in need. Shelters, food banks, help with utility bills, help with medical expenses, and temporary housing is offered in each state and or county. United Way may be able to help and provide a list of agencies within the area that will aid.

Local churches often have food gift cards, food pantries, or other services available for those who request help. They usually have a listing of other resources to help those who do not have basic needs.

Not all communities are the same nor are the resources within a given community the same. However, the first thing to do is to identify those resources that might be available.

- *State department of education.* Determine if there are funds, materials, or agencies that might help with specific needs to include educational materials, supplies, moneys, or books. Teachers must be resourceful in their search for items to help students learn and provide for their basic needs.
- *District.* Talk with district personnel to determine any special help that may be available if your school is among a few in the district with greater needs than the others.
- *Fast food.* Visit fast-food chains to see if they would sponsor reading, writing, or math programs with coupons, free food, etc. as initiatives to motivate students and earn food with good report card.
- *Hardware stores.* Gardens, science supplies, and art projects need materials that may be donated or provided at a substantial discount.
- *Grocery stores.* Snacks are so important to students. Find out if the stores can donate any surplus food.
- *Federal funding or grants.* Solicit educators in the schools or friends who have been successful grant writers. Do not be afraid to try writing for yourself. Do a little research to

determine those areas where grants are available. Be creative in your suggestions but be specific, use innovation ideas, and achievement goals.

- *Flea markets.* Visit flea markets, thrift shops, and garage sales for materials to supply science and art areas.
- *Local physicians.* Solicit the assistant of the medical field (dentists, general practitioners, optometrists, or pediatric physicians) to donate a day to conduct free dental checks, medical exams, or visual exams.

Resources for English Language Learners

National Center for Education Statistics ("The Condition of Education"), https://nces.ed.gov/programs/coe/indicator_cgf.asp.

English Language Learners in your state, https://www.npr.org/sections/ed/2017/02/23/512451228/5-million-english-language-learners-a-vast-pool-of-talent-at-risk.

REFERENCES

2018. *20 Simple Assessment Strategies You Can Use Every Day.* https://www.teachthought.com/pedagogy/20-simple-assessment-strategies-can-use-every-day/.

Akhtar, A. 2019. *20 photos that show how much being a school teacher has changed in the last 50 years.* https://www.businessinsider.com/how-public-school-teacher-changed-the-last-50-years-2019-7.

Adams, C. 2019. 11 Essential Strategies in Teaching Math. https://www.weareteachers.com/strategies-in-teaching-mathematics/.

American Academy of Pediatrics. 2018. *Which Kids are at Highest Risk for Suicide?* https://www.healthychildren.org/English/health-issues/conditions/emotional-problems/Pages/Which-Kids-are-at-Highest-Risk-for-Suicide.aspx.

Bradbury, Bruce, Jenkins, Stephen P., and Micklewright, John. 2000. *Child Poverty Dynamics in Seven Nations.* Innocenti Working Paper, No. 78 Florence: UNICEF Innocenti Research Centre.

Burgess, D. 2012. *Teach Like a Pirate: Increase Student Engagement, Boost Your Creativity, and Transform Your Life as an Educator.* San Diego, California: Dave Burgess Consulting, Inc.

Children's Defense Fund. 2018. *Child Poverty in America 2017: National Analysis.* https://www.childrensdefense.org/wp-content/uploads/2018/09/Child-Poverty-in-America-2017-National-Fact-Sheet.pdf.

Cook, H.A. 2015. *Beyond the Bars: One Woman's Journey to True Freedom.* Columbia, South Carolina: Kingdom Builders Publications LLC.

Cox, J. 2016. *What Are the Characteristics Every 21st-Century Teacher Should Have?* https://www.thoughtco.com/characteristics-of-a-21st-century-teacher-2081448.

Defining Homelessness. http://www.housingaccess.net/defining-home-lessness.html#homelessness.

Defining moment. 2020. https://www.dictionary.com/browse/defining-moment. Used in conjunction with Random House Unabridged Dictionary.

Dobrin, A. 2012. *The Effects of Poverty on the Brain, Psychology Today.*

Dobrin, A. 2012. *The Effects of Poverty on the Brain.* https://www.psychologytoday.com/us/blog/am-i-right/201210/the-effects-poverty-the-brain.

Envision. 2020. *5 Things Your Kids Should Focus on This Year.* https://www.Envisionexperience.com/blog/5-things-your-kids-should-focus-on-this-year.

Federal Register. 2019. *Annual Update of the HHS Poverty Guidelines* (Chart). https://www.federalregister.gov/documents/2019/02/01/2019-00621/annual-update-of-the-hhs-poverty-guidelines.

Fisher, D., and Frey, N. 2008. *Better Learning Through Structured Teaching: A Framework for the Gradual Release of Responsibility.* Alexandria, Virginia: ASCD.

Fox News (television series episode). 2019. *Ben Carson: California's "misguided concept of compassion" not helping homeless.*

Frequently Asked Questions. https://nhchc.org/understanding-homelessness/faq/.

Ginott, H. A quote by Haim G. Ginott. https://www.goodreads.com/quotes/81938-i-ve-come-to-a-frightening-conclusion-that-i-am-the.

Gonzalez, J. 2014. *12 Ways to Support English Learners in the Mainstream Classroom.* https://www.cultofpedagogy.com/supporting-esl-students-mainstream-classroom/.

Great Schools Partnership. 2016. 21st century skills definition. https://www.edglossary.org/21st-century-skills/

Hannaford, C. 1995. *Smart Moves: Why Learning is Not All in Your Head.* Arlington, Virginia: Great River Books.

Harmon, W. 2019. *5 Concrete Ways to Help Students Living in Poverty.* https://theartofeducation.edu/2018/09/11/5-concrete-ways-to-help-students-living-in-poverty/.

Heick, T. 2019. *10 Ways Teaching Has Changed in the Last 10 Years.* https://www.teachthought.com/the-future-of-learning/7-ways-teaching-has-changed/

Homeless in California Statistics. Homeless Estimation by State. US Interagency Council on Homelessness. 2018. https://www.usich.gov/homelessness-statistics/ca/.

Ingram, A. 2010. *6 Tips for Teaching in a Diverse Classroom.* https://www.imaginelearning.com/blog/2010/06/esl_struggling-readers-2.

Jensen, E. 2008. *Brain-Based Learning: The New Paradigm of Teaching* (2nd ed.). Thousand Oaks, California: Corwin Press.

Jensen, E. 2010. *Teaching with Poverty in Mind: What Being Poor Does to Kids' Brains and What Schools Can Do About It.* Alexandria, Virginia: ASCD.

Jensen, E. 2016. *Poor Students, Rich Teaching: Mindsets for Change.* Bloomington, Indiana: Solution Tree.

Karges-Bone, L. 2016. *Rich Brain, Poor Brain: Bridging Social and Synaptic Gaps in Schools.* Dayton, Ohio: Lorenz Educational Press.

Kennedy, M.Z. *10 Reasons Why Teachers Are Quitting Education.* https://vocal.media/education/10-reasons-why-teachers-are-quitting-education.

Labayen, D. 2019. *5 Ways to Fight Poverty.* http://file:///C:/Users/dotha/OneDrive/Desktop/Most%20Recent%20Book%2010%2010/Research%20for%20Book/5%20Ways%20to%20Fig.

Luby, J.L. 2015. *Poverty's Most Insidious Damage. JAMA Pediatrics, 169*(9), 810. doi:10.1001/jamapediatrics.2015.1682.

Luby, J., Belden, A., Botteron, K., Marrus, N., Harms, M.P., Babbs, C., and Barch, D. 2013. *The Effects of Poverty on Childhood Brain Development. JAMA Pediatrics, 167(12), 1135.* doi:10.1001/jamapediatrics.2013.3139.

Mercer, T. 2019. *Values in Today's Society.* https://youthfirstinc.org/values-in-todays-society/.

McClain, M. 2015. *5 Ways to Help Students Affected by Generational Poverty.* https://www.edutopia.org/discussion/5-ways-help-students-affected-generational-poverty.

McTighe, J., and Willis, J. 2019. *Upgrade Your Teaching: Understanding by Design Meets Neuroscience*. Alexandria, Virginia: ASCD.

New York University. 2017. *Multicultural awareness boosts teaching competency, but is an uneven resource among future teachers: Prior experience working with youth of color linked to more multicultural awareness. ScienceDaily*. November 3, 2019 from www.sciencedaily.com/releases/2017/12/171205091458.htm.

Newmann, J., and Mucciolo, L. 2017. *Poor Kids* (video file). https.//www.pbs.org/wgbh/frontline/film/poor-kids/.

Neuman, S.B., and Celano, D.C. 2015. *Giving Our Children a Fighting Chance: Poverty, Literacy, and the Development of Information Capital*. New York, New York: Teachers College Press.

Noble et al, K.G. 2017. *Family Income, Parental Education, and Brain Structure in Children and Adolescents. Nature Neuroscience, 18.* https://blogs.scientificamerican.com/sa-visual/this-is-your-brain-on-poverty/.

Payne, R.K. 1998. *A Framework for Understanding Poverty*. Highlands, Texas: Aha Process.

Payne, R.K., DeVol, P. E., and Smith, T. D. 2006. *Bridges Out of Poverty: Strategies for Professionals and Communities (Workbook)*. Highlands, Texas: Aha Process.

Poverty Rate by State. 2019. http://worldpopulationreview.com/states/poverty-rate-by-state/.

Publishing, H. 2017. *These 18 Practices are Proven Effective for Teaching Reading*. https://medium.com/@heinemann/these-18-practices-are-proven-effective-for-teaching-reading-5ea6c-9424fa0.

Robinson, N.J. 2018. *There Is No Teacher Shortage. Current Affairs*.

Rumberger, R.W. 2013. *Poverty and high school dropouts, the impact of family and community poverty on high school dropouts. American Psychological Association.* https://www.apa.org/pi/ses/resources/indicator/2013/05/poverty-dropouts.

Sheftall, A.H., Asti, L., Horowitz, L.M., Felts, A., Fontanella, C.A., Campo, J.V., and Bridge, J.A. 2016. *Suicide in Elementary-*

School-Aged Children and Early Adolescents. Pediatrics, 138(4), e20160436. doi:10.1542/peds.2016-0436.

St. Francis of Assisi National Shrine: Franciscan Prayer. http://www.shrinesf.org/franciscan-prayer.html.

Stallen, M.M. 2017. *Poverty and the Developing Brain.* https://behavioralscientist.org/can-neuroscientists-help-us-understand-fight-effects-childhood-poverty/.

Stallen, M.M. 2017. *Poverty and the Developing Brain. Society.* https://behavioralscientist.org/can-neuroscientists-help-us-understand-fight-effects-childhood-poverty/.

US Census Bureau. 2019. *Poverty.* https://www.census.gov/topics/income-poverty/poverty.html.

Vallas, R., and Boteach, M. 2014. *The Top 10 Solutions to Cut Poverty and Grow the Middle Class.* https://www.americanprogress.org/issues/poverty/news/2014/09/17/97287/the-top-10-solutions-to-cut-poverty-and-grow-the-middle-class/.

What Causes Homelessness? 2016. https://endhomelessness.org/homelessness-in-america/what-causes-homelessness/.

What the role of Society is in today's world? 2012. http://www.preservearticles.com/education/what-the-role-of-society-is-in-todays-world/22867.

Zadina, J. 2014. *Multiple Pathways to the Student Brain: Energizing and Enhancing Instruction.* Hoboken, New Jersey: John Wiley & Sons.

Zemelman, S., Daniels, H., and Hyde, A.A. 2005. *Best Practice: Today's Standards for Teaching and Learning in America's Schools* (3rd ed.). Portsmouth, New Hampshire: Heinemann.

"10 Years. 180 School Shootings. 356 Victims." CNN—Breaking News, Latest News and Videos. Accessed March 23, 2020. https://www.cnn.com/interactive/2019/07/us/ten-years-of-school-shootings-trnd/.

"6 Ways the Climate Changed Over the Past Decade." World Resources Institute. Last modified January 7, 2020. https://www.wri.org/blog/2019/12/6-ways-climate-changed-over-past-decade.

"Global Warming Influence on Extreme Weather Events Has Been Frequently Underestimated." ScienceDaily. Last modified

March 24, 2020. https://www.sciencedaily.com/releases/2020/03/200318143722.htm.

"History of School Shootings in the United States." K12 Academics | Your Nationwide Resource for Everything Education. Accessed March 23, 2020. https://www.k12academics.com/school-shootings/history-school-shootings-united-states.

Jarus, Owen. "20 of the Worst Epidemics and Pandemics in History." Livescience.com. Last modified March 20, 2020. https://www.livescience.com/worst-epidemics-and-pandemics-in-history.html.

"Lockdown Vs Lockout." LockOut | Advanced Building Lockout Systems. Last modified October 17, 2019. https://lockoutusa.com/lockdown-vs-lockout/.

"Pandemics in the Last 100 Years Search." Google. Accessed March 23, 2020. https://www.google.com/search?q=pandemics+in+the+last+100+years&oq=pandemics+in+th&aqs=chrome.0.0j69i57j0l6.9021j0j8&sourceid=chrome&ie=UTF-8.

ABOUT THE AUTHOR

Having taught for over thirty-five years in public education, Dr. Doris Hawkins is familiar with teaching children with a variety of abilities from varied backgrounds with many different needs. Her personal experience in difficult situations as a child allows her to have both empathy, insights, and sympathy for some of the children in hard situations.

Being a lifelong learner, Dr. Hawkins continues to learn, and through this, ongoing learning has added to her already earned certification in elementary education and multiple areas of special education with a certification in early childhood. In addition, she is among the first in the country to receive certification in teaching children of poverty. Her degrees are in elementary education (Bachelor of Arts and Doctor of Philosophy) and special education (Master of Education in generic special education).

Throughout her teaching career, Dr. Hawkins worked with student teachers, helping them complete the final phase of the requirements for teaching. In doing so, she saw the challenges that newcomers to the profession encounter. She guided those who struggled to prayerfully consider what is really a "good fit" and celebrated with those who immediately loved the profession and demonstrated a talent for it. In addition, Dr. Hawkins has taught at the college level (at the University of South Carolina) and continues to teach at North Greenville University.

As a Christian, Doris reveals times when God's hand helped her make a significant difference in the lives of others. Her close walk with God has afforded her the opportunity to utilize the power of God coupled with the power that teachers have to help students and other teachers be successful. Having taught so many different children allows Doris to speak with authority from firsthand experience, providing practical classroom applications to help teachers be effective educators in an ever-changing society.

CPSIA information can be obtained
at www.ICGtesting.com
Printed in the USA
FSHW010158011020
74247FS